Confessions of an

Air Traffic Controller

*An Autobiography of
Adventure, Humor, Lack of Talent, and
Terror by a Unique Aviator*

DANNY MORTENSEN

ISBN 978-1-64299-912-9 (paperback)
ISBN 978-1-64299-913-6 (digital)

Christian Faith Publishing, Inc.
832 Park Avenue
Meadville, PA 16335
www.christianfaithpublishing.com

Printed in the United States of America

Dedicated to my children, Tye and Litsa.

Later in life, questions arose about the family history. We live busy lives and don't think of those things when we are young.

Looking through the family photos, I wondered *Who are these people?* No names on the back, no dates—a mystery. Obviously, they were important; however, their stories are lost to time.

This is my legacy for my children and grandchildren. Both are to be commended for their lifestyles and successes. They grew up with kids in school who got into trouble, did drugs, and yet, they resisted the temptation to fall from grace in the eyes of the Lord. Both have a master's degree and are gainfully employed. Cheryl and I are both so proud of them and our three grandchildren, Paige, Areli, and Clara, ages three, two, and three months, respectively.

Cheryl, Tye, Litsa, Danny, and Grandpa Ernie

Contents

Foreword

Competitive air race pilot, aerobatic pilot, former air traffic controller, flight instructor, airplane owner, successful businessman, radio show host, airline instructor, and raconteur; these are just a few of the entries in the curriculum vitae of my friend, Danny Mortensen. Danny also happens to be the author and chief confessor of this wonderful book titled *Confessions of an Air Traffic Controller*.

Had I known that hearing confessions was so much fun, I would have applied to a Jesuit Monastery right out of high school. These confessions, however, aren't the submissions offered as atonement for our sins. Instead, they are what I call "darn good stories," and you need not wear a hooded robe to be entertained by them (unless you want to, of course).

Danny Mortensen is clearly the heir to a long line of Indiana Jones-like aviators—individuals with a knack for finding adventure every time they step into the cockpit of an airplane. Don't get me wrong. Swashbuckling, crystal skulls, and crazed natives play no part in these confessional narratives. Yet, if we calibrate the range of everyday emotions, from boredom to high adventure, Danny always nudges himself toward the latter end of that spectrum. When he does, he almost always manages to land upright, unscathed, and well-groomed. Like every one of us, however, Danny occasionally steps in it. Unlike most of us, when he does, it makes for a darn good story.

I advise you to strap yourself tightly into your recliner before you read about Danny's 200 mph crash at Reno in the AMSOIL Rutan Racer. It's just like being there without actually being there. After accidentally slipping into the wake of a preceding race plane, Danny's airplane turned into a lawn dart. Cartwheeling along the

9

desert floor, he somehow managed to exit the wreckage upright, unscathed, and looking relatively intact. The only casualty was a one-time six-foot saguaro cactus that stood at one foot tall after the accident. I made up that last sentence, but only because I suspect it's true. Good golly! I'll bet Indiana Jones has never done that—okay, maybe he came close.

If you stoked the fires of your imagination, could you ever conceive of a situation where air traffic controllers worked naked in a tower cab? Well, it happened at San Jose tower. When I read Danny's "Garden of Eden" tower story, I darn near fell off my chair because I was laughing so hard. All I could think of was that this man knows how to turn an ordinary experience into a memorable adventure.

When you read *Confessions of an Air Traffic Controller*, you'll come away with the impression that Danny has a deep respect and love for his fellow man. He certainly enjoys being around people that love what they do—especially if this involves airplanes—and he shows it. His most unique gift, in my opinion, is his sense of playfulness. Fortunately, he's smart and wise enough to know how to make the most of his everyday aviation experience and do so safely (most of the time).

I know you'll enjoy reading *Confessions of an Air Traffic Controller* as much as I did.

Rod Machado
San Clemente, CA 2018

Introduction

I grew up listening to World War II stories told by my dad, Ernie, who was an aviation mechanic in the Navy. He was on the battleship USS *Mississippi* (BN-41) off Iceland on convoy duty on December 7, 1941. One of his secondary duties was passing up five inch antiaircraft shells to the gun platform. The Germans would shadow the convoys with their long range four-engine Condor bombers and transmit the information to their U-boats.

The gun crew would throw the heavy, empty five inch shell casings over the side, and one casing hit dad in the head, knocking him out. While in the ship's hospital, he contracted pneumonia and was laid up for two weeks. As a result, he developed Parkinson's disease, which was diagnosed after the war resulting in a 100 percent disability. If you saw him walking down the street, you might think he was drunk. Everybody liked dad and his stories. In spite of his handicap, he was able to get around and would spend mornings drinking coffee with the old-timers in the country drug store in Loomis, California, just outside of Sacramento.

He also served on two baby flattops in the Pacific. It was in Chicago on a trolley while home on leave that he met Katherine "Katy" Saites, a 20-year-old half-Greek, half-Ukrainian gal, and they married in 1944. After the war, they moved to Flint, Michigan, where my Greek grandfather, John Saites, had several restaurants. I grew up in Danny's Grill with one hand in the cash register for comic books and the other hand in the ice cream cooler.

Dad had a wonderful sense of humor and a big smile and would recite his Navy stories several times each day. We four kids, Anna, Suzie, Johnny, and myself, would hold up a hand behind his back to signify to the others how many times that day we had heard that one. If you didn't know history, you would have thought Dad had won WWII single-handedly. His escapades are probably where I got my sense of mischief. The acorn doesn't fall far from the tree.

We would visit his parents, German immigrants, in the summers by driving from Michigan to Arizona. It was there that I fell in love with airplanes. The Stearman crop dusters were busy over the cotton fields, and the sound of jet fighters overhead from Luke Air Force Base were music to my ears.

Following graduation from Arizona State University in January 1969, I served a two-year tour of duty as an infantry officer (inspired by Dad) and then was hired by the FAA as an air traffic controller. I had obtained a private pilot certificate while at ASU, and with the GI Bill, I went on to obtain all the subsequent certificates, culminating in an Air Transport Pilot (ATP) certificate—the most coveted of all FAA tickets. Here is the rest of the story of lessons learned in pursuit of fame and fortune . . .

Chapter 1

The Early Years

June 1964–January 1969, Arizona State University

The Engineering Department at ASU offered an air navigation course and a private pilot course. I took advantage of this opportunity in 1966 as a sophomore. I paid $10 per hour for the aircraft rental, which included fuel and the instructor. The airlines were hiring, and I went through five instructors while working on my certificate.

My first solo at Falcon Field in Mesa, AZ was a surprise. I wasn't expecting the instructor to hop out and tell me to take the Cessna 150 around the pattern by myself. Although confident, I was still a little apprehensive yet excited. On my first touch-and-go on that single runway, I forgot to retract full flaps and wondered why the aircraft wouldn't climb. Then I remembered the flaps and cleared the power lines at the far end of the field. I passed my private pilot check ride on June 11, 1968 at Deer Valley Airport in Phoenix.

I soon discovered that girls were inclined to accept a date if I mentioned flying to lunch or dinner I was hooked and spent my entire life in aviation. Flying is a hard way to make an easy living.

My major at ASU was the Russian language. I had an advantage for the first week because I knew the Cyrillic alphabet. Then it got challenging. I debated switching to a business major the second semester, but the gal sitting next to me, Carol Tessitore, was a cute blonde and head cheerleader who kept asking me for help, and she said she was taking Russian 102 the next semester.

I originally was an anthropology major. I signed up for Air Force ROTC because I wanted to fly. They talked me into changing my major to Russian. You need 20/20 for pilot training, and at the end of my sophomore year, my eyes had deteriorated to 20/50. That was good enough for Army ROTC, so I switched. Army aviators were selected from the infantry branch, but by the time I was sworn in, my eyes were 20/100. I became an infantry lieutenant with no wings.

While playing intramural football at ASU, I tore cartilage in the left knee. I had surgery at the Mayo Clinic in Rochester, Minnesota, but the knee was never the same again. The Army offered to release me from my two year obligation, but I was instilled with a sense of pride for this country, unlike many of my peers who were protesting against our involvement in Viet Nam.

I taught 8th grade at an elementary school in Loomis, California for a year while recovering from surgery. My little brother, John, was in my class.

I accepted my commission at the Presidio in San Francisco in 1969 with Dad at my side. It was a proud moment for both of us. My tour of duty was spent at Ft. Ord, California. One of my collateral duties was as a post burial officer. It was a difficult assignment, and I managed to hold back the tears when the bugler sounded "Taps," the rifle salute took place, and I presented the flag to the next of kin on behalf of a grateful nation.

Chapter 2

Reid-Hillview Airport (RHV), San Jose, California

I was released from active duty in December 1971 and made captain in the Reserves. Arriving home, I was going through some boxes and found the telegram from the FAA offering me a position two years earlier. I had actually forgotten about it. I called, and the offer was still valid.

June 28, 1973, the Start of My FAA Career

The FAA hired me as an air traffic controller. My first assignment was Reid-Hillview, a satellite airport in San Jose. I did all of my training there, and toward the end of my probationary year, the FAA finally had funds to send me to the FAA Academy in Oklahoma City, Oklahoma for two weeks of indoctrination.  Normally, you would go there first before reporting to your first facility. There wasn't anything challenging about the training, having already finished my on-the-job (OJT) training at Reid-Hillview.

It was October and the usual order of business at the Academy was an 8 a.m. showtime for class. The instructor would take attendance and then tell us to take a 10-minute break and be back at 1 p.m.

We spent most of our time watching the World Series on TV at the Holiday Inn with Reggie Jackson (ASU) hitting home runs.

My First Time on Local Control

I'd been in the FAA for about two months observing the journeymen. I was a pilot, but they always picked the slowest period to put you on the air the first time. It was late evening. My instructor, Thurmon Gupton, told me to take a seat and work some traffic. All FAA facilities are training sites.

The airport was quiet; no traffic. Thurm was reading a pocket novel sitting next to me, and I waited nervously for my first call. I only got one call that night; a gal 10 miles south, inbound for landing. I stumbled through the format and told her to report two mile final. Then I noticed her wingtip lights were reversing position. She was doing rolls on final at night. I told Thurm. He had recognized the voice and, without even looking up, said "Oh, that's just Amelia (Reid); she's an institution here." Welcome to Reid-Hillview Airport. The system wasn't much different anywhere else.

"Go Around" Miscommunication

I was busy working both runways, 31R and 31L, when I noticed the twin Cessna on final had not extended his landing gear. I advised him "no gear" and continued working ten aircraft in the closed traffic pattern on Runway 31 Right and the itinerant departures and inbounds on Runway 31 Left. The supervisor noticed the twin on final and tapped me on the shoulder saying "no gear." "Ya, I'll tell 'em again." The pilot acknowledged both of my transmissions, but apparently, what I was saying was not registering. The supervisor jumped on the frequency and yelled at him to "go around," but the pilot didn't have his ears on. He touched down, sliding to a stop, gear up on the runway.

I reached for the red phone, a direct line to the fire department on the field, and issued instructions to the next aircraft. It was a student solo in a Cessna 150, and I said, "Go around, aircraft on run-

way," as per the controller handbook and went back to my other traffic. The supervisor tapped me on the shoulder and said "tell 'em to go
around." I reissued the instruction, and again, the student acknowledged. The supervisor then yelled at the student on the frequency,
but he touched down on the painted runway numbers, taxied up to
the disabled twin, then around him, and took off again.

The ATC phrase "go around, aircraft on the runway" meant
he was to overfly the runway at 500 feet. It just wasn't my day. His
classroom instruction had not covered the phrase. His instructor had
told him two touch-and-go's and then a full stop. We call this a "deal"
in the FAA.

Another Student Solo

The supervisor got a call from an instructor at one of the flight
schools on the other side of the field. He was sending a student out
for his first solo and requesting two touch-and-go's and then a full
stop. The supervisor, Bill Brown, gave the ground controller, Greg
Hildebrand, the request along with the tail number. It was a busy
hour, and when Greg had a chance, he mentioned to the local controller working Runway 31R that there was a "virgin" (nonstandard
phraseology) in Cessna 23B coming his way.

The local controller, Greg Hopkins, assumed it was a gal.
About 15 minutes later, the student called Greg number two on
his frequency, having worked his way to the number one spot on
the taxiway for takeoff. The student did not state a request for two
touch-and-go's and a full stop. Greg was keyed up for a female voice.
Assuming the male pilot wanted a straight out departure, he cleared
him to cross the first runway and hold short of the second, parallel
runway, 31L.

I was working the itinerant runway, 31L. The student then
called me on my frequency, holding short of my runway, and again,
did not state his request. The internal chain of communication had
been broken. I had no idea he wanted to stay in the traffic pattern.
I built a hole for a straight out departure among my arrivals and
launched him.

About 15 minutes later, the student called me on five-mile final, having flown a huge B52 type traffic pattern around the east side of the airport. I sequenced him number four to follow a Cessna ahead on four-mile final. At the appropriate time, I cleared him to land.

Still no word from the student about a touch-and-go. They say a student pilot on his first solo is more stressed than a fighter pilot in combat. Now, I haven't flown combat, but I do remember my first date. You get the picture.

The student touched down and lost control of his C150, departed the runway, and headed across the grass directly at the control tower. He came to a stop when he encountered the chain-link fence around the building. A damaged airplane and an injured student, all due to miscommunication on both sides of the microphone.

Operating Initials

Controllers have operating initials, and we close out our internal messages to each other with our initials (for the record). All of our communications are taped. I chose DM, and of course, the journeymen would then come up with a moniker to fit the trainees (all in the spirit of good-natured ribbing). I soon acquired "Dum Mother," and my roommate, Greg Hopkins, was HS (Horse S---). Robert Williams, a journeyman controller, was RW, and he was referred to as "Rain Showers" (the National Weather Service weather abbreviation).

RW Gets Lost

Robert was a private pilot and would rent a C150 from one of the flight schools across the field and fly around for an hour to maintain currency on his days off. Bob knew all the local landmarks because we controllers would take the weather observation each hour based on known landmarks visible to us from the tower.

On this particular day, it was restricted visibility due to the morning haze, requiring a Special VFR (Visual Flight Rules) procedure to depart and arrive at the airport. Special VFR means a ceiling of less than 1,000 feet and/or visibility less than 3 miles. We actually had just over 1 mile of visibility. You could look straight down and see the ground, but horizontal visibility was virtually nonexistent, even though the sun was filtering through the haze.

I was working the traffic when RW called for a clearance back into the control zone. When the departing aircraft was reported clear of the control zone by Departure Control (radar), I cleared RW with instructions to report entering downwind. Another four aircraft then called in succession, wanting to return from the student practice area to the east of the airport. They all reported having each other in sight, and so I had a daisy chain of five aircraft inbound with RW in the lead.

Several minutes went by, and I asked RW for his position. He was overdue. The other four aircraft were trusting him to lead them to the airport. He finally admitted he was lost. The supervisor called San Jose Tower some six miles northwest and told them to suspend operations until we figured out where RW and his flock were located. RW finally figured it out after lots of chatter on the frequency from the other four aircraft. It took about 20 minutes before we were able to restore commercial operations at San Jose International across town.

Formal Attire Required

The FAA was different in the early 1970s. Neckties were required and no blue jeans, even though we normally did not have contact with the public. My roommate, Greg Hopkins, and I were trainees and always getting into trouble. One day, while working traffic at Reid-Hillview, Greg, who was on a break, reached around from behind me and cut my tie off with a scissors. Bill Brown, the supervisor, came unglued. He put Greg on the position and sent me home to get another necktie, stating angrily, "You can't work the position without a tie." We wore the ugliest ties that didn't match our shirts just to irritate management.

ATC System Shuts Down

It was Christmas rush. Each facility has a FDEP (Flight Data Entry and Printout) machine which types out the instrument clearances. This is the only position you can trust a trainee unsupervised. They can't screw it up. I asked the maintenance technician servicing the machine how he would send a test message. He said the little known computer code entry was ACTDO. After he left, I typed "Merry Xmas." It shut down the entire system in the Western Region while every FDEP computer printed the salutation repeatedly for five minutes. A maintenance tech at Oakland Center in Fremont, California finally managed to override the command.

The tower chief got his butt chewed by Region when the message was traced back to our tower, but management never figured out who done it. Controllers did not have access to that maintenance code, let alone a trainee.

Here, Let Me Help You

RHV Tower had some colorful characters. The old farts used to tell some amazing stories. I learned a lot from Joe L'Argent and ol' "Sarge" Thompson. We rookies stood in awe of our instructors until the day we discovered that they were human.

It was a cold winter morning, and we had some lady visitors from the Ninety-Nines, an organization of women pilots. As one of the ladies began to take off her heavy coat, RW, working local control, turned to help her. Alas, in his haste to assist, he grabbed her coat and her blouse and removed both from her lovely body.

RW turned bright red and lost the picture as far as traffic was concerned. The rest of us were rolling on the floor while the supervisor ushered the lady downstairs to an office to get dressed. She didn't seem embarrassed by the commotion, but it was a good five minutes before order (and safety) was restored. Unfortunately, that was the last year the 99s brought us cookies for Christmas.

Hey DM, Phone Call for Ya

When you finally qualify on all the positions, the journeymen give you more than your share of work while they sip coffee and chitchat in the back of the tower cab. RHV was a busy little airport ranked 26th in the world with two parallel runways. I was busy working on a 100-hour traffic count.

The supervisor, Bill Newman, handed me the telephone with a silly grin on his face and says it's for me. What? They usually took a message. I told him I was busy and to leave me alone. He insisted I take the call. This was unheard of and against the rules.

It was an aircraft east of airport calling on his portable phone for landing instructions. The poor guy had been holding for 20 minutes and had not been able to get a word in on the frequency due to heavy traffic. Whoever heard of a phone in a Cessna back in 1974? I didn't believe the pilot at first, and everybody got a good laugh out of that one at my expense.

The Best Controller I Ever Met

My roommate for the first two years in the FAA was Greg Hopkins. Greg was a former Army controller who served in 'Nam, owned a C150, and was not mentally challenged by the complexity of the ATC system. He had almost total recall and would amaze management by working local control combining both runways at RHV without a pencil and pad to record the aircraft call signs, types, and positions. Management had to confer to discuss the rationale of allowing Greg to work without writing anything down on paper.

What was their liability if something happened? It was a big crisis for them. In the end, Greg was allowed to work the way he wanted. It always amazed the pilots to hear Greg exchange traffic because he would add the aircraft color which the local pilots had not given, and we had 450 aircraft based there.

The Trainee

The FAA had a separate ATC hiring list of disadvantaged minorities. They would send them to the FAA Academy at Oklahoma City to learn reading and writing and then to the ATC facilities for OJT. We got a black gal who simply could not control traffic. Her trainer refused to sign her off, but management did. Kind of scary that we had people with so little talent controlling traffic simply to increase the minority numbers in the FAA workforce.

The Tunnel

Greg and I would take his C150 and fly off on occasional weekends, but our schedules were generally different. Greg wanted to go home to Southern California for a long weekend, but his time off started one day later than mine. He asked me to take the Cessna home to Sacramento for my weekend, and he called in sick on his last day.

It was April 23, 1974. I told the tower crew I'd be in the C150 after work and headed for Sacramento, and Greg squeezed in and out of sight. After takeoff and out of sight of the airport, we reversed course and headed south to Los Angeles.

Greg asked if I knew the route. I said yes and assumed he knew it. It began to rain that evening. We were down on Highway 101 at 500 feet north of Lompoc in a canyon. We came around a hill, and the road ended in a tunnel. A quick 180-degree turn and back to the Lompoc Airport we went.

The fuel gauges were down to a quarter of the tank. Then Greg said he didn't trust the gauges. I'm fearless, but this comment upset

me. I had used his C150 in the past, and he never said anything about this. He reminded me that I had said I knew the route, and I said, "Yes, but not at 500 feet."

Sitting in the airport cafe for dinner, two California Highway Patrolmen were talkin' to the waitress about a search in the canyon. Someone had seen us and thought we had crashed. Oops.

Tailwheel Checkout

I received my tailwheel endorsement at RHV. On one of the training flights, my instructor and I were in a single-engine Citabria. On takeoff, the butterfly mechanism in the carburetor intake broke, and we experienced a partial loss of power. Declaring an emergency, we limped around the pattern at with just enough power to clear the power lines on the east side. Just another day at RHV.

Ice

Oakland Center called us with an emergency inbound. A Cessna 182 had picked up a load of ice while flying in the clouds one winter day and could not maintain altitude. We were the closest airport. The Cessna broke out of the low clouds at several hundred feet on final, and we could see sheets of ice breaking off and falling into the parking lot at Eastridge Shopping Center directly across the street. The warmer air below was melting the ice.

Student Lands Short of the Runway

One student suffered carburetor ice on final and landed on the roof of the Eastridge Shopping Center. No serious damage to the aircraft, but the student was so perplexed that he almost ran off the roof when he exited the Aeronca Champ. The flight school had to dismantle the airplane and take it down the stairs to remove it from the roof.

My First Airplane

Greg and I both wanted to build multiengine time in our logbooks. We were keeping the airline option in our back pockets. I was looking for something unique. There was a twin-engine WWII trainer for sale—an AT17 Bobcat affectionately known as a "bamboo bomber." It had big radial Jacobs engines and wooden spars in the wings. The aircraft was about 35 years old, and they had a history of catching fire (in flight). Greg got cold feet, and I couldn't afford it without him.

Then I heard of a single-engine Stearman biplane, another WWII trainer, for $5000 on the airport. By the time I got off work and around to the other side of the airport, it had been sold. Today, they sell for about $100,000.

A few months later in October of 1974, I learned of a single-seat Smith Miniplane hidden away in a hangar. The builder had arranged for someone to test fly it since he had lost his medical. It had been sitting for two years. I fell in love with it. It was an open cockpit biplane with an electrical system, a smoke tank, and a tailwheel.

Anybody can fly a tricycle type (nose wheel) aircraft. Real pilots fly taildraggers. The Bank of America agreed to finance it, and I bought it for $5000.

On my first flight, I nearly crashed back on to the runway on takeoff. I sat a little tall in the cockpit with a radio headset on my ears. The slipstream ripped the headset off my head, and it was bouncing outside the cockpit against the fuselage. I was trying to pull it back in while keeping one hand on the control stick, and the aircraft nosed back down to the runway while my attention was diverted. I looked forward and managed to pull full aft on the control stick actually doing a touch-and-go on the runway. That was close.

Another second and I would have hit hard and collapsed the landing gear, destroying the aircraft and probably myself, or at least my aviation career. Of course, everyone in the tower was watching and wondering what was happening. The rest of the flight was uneventful.

I commuted home to Sacramento in the Smith and logged over 240 hours in it. It was truly a step back to the golden age of aviation in the twenties and thirties when man confronted Mother Nature while wearing a scarf and goggles in an open cockpit. It is indescribable to be in command of such a beautiful ship, but it led to a mindset of invincibility, a dangerous attitude that I could deal with fog, clouds, winds, and rain just like the old airmail pilots.

You would think the experiences that followed would be humbling, but as each challenge was met, it increased my confidence that I could deal with anything. I was going to learn a few lessons over the next several years with this attitude.

The 360

I returned from Sacramento one Saturday morning into the traffic pattern to start my work week. It was raining. Journeyman Joe L'Argent was takin' bets I would call in sick.

There was only one airplane on four-mile final, so RW gave me a 360-degree turn to follow the Cessna on long final. I couldn't resist the temptation. I was high and descending into the traffic pattern fast and knew there were no other aircraft in the area based on radio traffic. I was a little upset because I could easily beat the Cessna on final and was now going to be late for work. Heck, I could be in the hangar before that traffic crossed the threshold.

I rogered his instruction and did a vertical 360 loop instead of the required horizontal turn. RW had kittens. It was a weekend so I knew tower chief wasn't in the tower, and I got away with it. The things we do when we're young and stupid.

An interesting thing about flying open cockpit in the rain: you don't get wet except for the top of your cloth helmet in the airflow above the windscreen. Taxiing in the rain is a different story. You get drenched.

A DC8 on Final

The runways at RHV Airport and San Jose International (SJC) were basically parallel. It was not unusual for inbound traffic to line up visually for the wrong airport. On one particular day, I had visual with a four-engine jet that appeared to be on my final. I asked SJC Tower on the hotline if they were missing a great big jet inbound to which they replied, "Yes, a Trans International Airlines DC8." I asked them to suggest a slight turn to the left to avoid overtaking my little guys on final. Our runways were only 3,100 feet and insufficient for a heavy passenger jet.

Now this would happen to our traffic too. You would think a general aviation airplane would be able to recognize the difference between our runways and the 11,000 feet of concrete at SJC. On one occasion, I asked a missing Cessna to verify he was on final for Reid-Hillview, to which he replied, "Ya, I recognize your voice." Dummy. It happened frequently enough that the FAA installed a direct line between the two control towers. Dialing on a commercial line didn't work if someone was using the phone.

How to Get Weekends Off

One of the controllers at San Jose (SJC) tower was tired of having days off which didn't match those with his wife. Oakland Center was hard up for controllers. They promised anyone who transferred with return rights to their previous facility if they failed to check out.

Well, it doesn't take a controller long to figure out how to beat the system. Our friend, who will remain anonymous, realized that while you are in training at the Center, you have weekends off. He got his weekends for one year and deliberately failed to check out, returning to SJC tower where he later became a supervisor.

Who Ate My Lunch?

The journeyman controllers would go through the sack lunches in the fridge in the break room and eat the good stuff. It was part of the hazing of new controllers. I finally resorted to taking my lunch to the tower cab to guard it.

Controllers are obnoxious and overassertive, but the camaraderie when it got busy was really great. You got a natural high as you rose to the challenge of heavy traffic. The barrage of sarcastic humor and practical jokes to relieve the stress was like the TV series *Mash*. Anything to irritate our stuffy, conservative managers was fair game.

Someone would unscrew the light bulb in the elevator so that it hung by a thread. When the elevator started moving, the bulb would drop and sound like a gunshot. The pictures hanging in the stairwell were frequently found upside down until the tower chief nailed 'em to the wall. The journeymen blamed it on a phantom pilot, and the supervisors blamed the trainees.

Obnoxious Management

Greg transferred to San Jose tower and told me this story. One of the San Jose tower supervisors had an annoying habit of coming in an hour early—around seven each morning—sitting in the back of the tower cab, drinking coffee. The three journeymen controllers on duty for the big airline push did not like this particular sup (or management in general). The crew decided they could be just as annoying and decided to put an end to their unwelcome visitor with a typical controller response.

One morning, they stripped stark naked except for their headsets and continued to work traffic. When the early bird came bounding up the steps . . . Well, you can imagine the look on his face. He hightailed back down the stairs and never showed up early again.

Near Miss

I was flying home to Sacramento in my bright yellow biplane from Reid. Hunkered down in the open cockpit at the appropriate altitude for an easterly heading at 5,500 feet over Tracy, CA, I began to feel a vibration. Was it the engine? The airframe? It was getting worse, and I'm scanning the instrument panel for an indication of imminent engine failure.

Then, over the top of me from behind passed a twin-engine aircraft, missing me by about 40 feet. His two propellers were out of sync and producing the vibration. I don't know how he missed seeing me. He must have had his head down in the cockpit not watching for traffic.

Shoot Down

Reid-Hillview has lots of houses on the west and north sides of the airport. Departures on the primary runways, 31L and 31R, pass directly over the homes to the north. We had an Aeronca Champ (65 HP), a slow climber, hit by an arrow on takeoff. It stuck in the fabric-covered wing, and the pilot immediately returned to the airport. Local police were dispatched to find the culprits, but the kids had long disappeared.

Garden City Aero

In November of 1974, Dad wanted to visit his sister in Phoenix, AZ, so I rented a Cessna 172 from the local flight school, Garden City Aero, with a planned fuel stop about halfway. I checked the aircraft the evening before at the FBO (Fixed Base Operator) and verified full fuel tanks. The next morning, we departed. I did not know that someone had flown the C172 during the middle of the night and did not refuel it. The fuel gauges were still on "full" when we left but minus about one hour of fuel. My mistake was not doing a proper preflight in the morning darkness.

Over the Los Angeles basin, the airports began to fog in about the time we arrived, and then I noticed the fuel gauges lower than they should be. We requested an IFR approach into the nearest airport with landing minimums—Long Beach Airport. We landed with less than a gallon of useable fuel. By the way, the air mile distance between both airports is only 346 miles. I learned that C172 fuel gauges were not all that accurate either.

Marion Barnick

One of the maintenance facilities on the Reid-Hillview Airport was Gee Bee Aero in the north corner of the field. It was owned by a wonderful lady by the name of Marion Barnick. I was a guest in her home on numerous occasions when I was dating a Trans International Airlines flight attendant who boarded there.

In November 1979, Marion took a vacation to New Zealand. While there, she bought a ticket on an Air New Zealand DC10 excursion flight from Auckland to overfly Antarctica on their popular sightseeing trip. Unfortunately, Flight 901 did not return. The pilots were given the wrong latitude/longitude coordinates by the dispatch office and descended in clouds to get under the overcast for the passengers to be able to see the continent. They hit Mt. Erebus on Ross Island hidden in the cloud. No survivors.

Moon Over San Jose

Several of the controllers from San Jose tower, including Greg Hopkins and Brian Metcalfe, were planning a departure from Reid-Hillview on a fishing trip to Oregon. As they were leaving on the same morning that I was starting my weekend, I decided to tag along in the Smith part of the way. The reason was the ground fog forming each morning, which closed the airport for VFR arrivals and departures, and my ship was not equipped for IFR (Instrument Flight Rules).

They were departing as a formation flight of four aircraft on an IFR flight plan. It was 5 a.m., well before sunrise but a full moon. I told them I would follow them on takeoff and, once above the fog, would turn right for Sacramento. By staying close to ship #4, I could follow his lights up through the fog.

It worked, but I realized, once aloft, that if they outran me, I only had the moon overhead for a reference. A moment of inspiration—if I survive this, I will never do this again! As time went by and memories fade, I would make the same mistake again. The lesson would be forgotten.

My CFI Checkride

I started my flight instructor training while at Reid-Hillview. I got off work at RHV and borrowed the C150 belonging to Greg. I flew six miles to SJC and walked into the FAA General Aviation District Office (GADO) and presented my credentials to Jack Hocker, along with the aircraft logbooks. Not more than 15 minutes later, my tower chief, Olin Young, called the GADO manager and told him to send me back to Reid-Hillview for mandatory overtime. They were short-staffed and needed me. Someone had called in sick. No problem, but it meant rescheduling my checkride some three weeks later.

On the second visit to the GADO, the same thing happened. The aviation gods were not looking favorably on me. I was recalled to Reed-Hillview after only 30 minutes with the inspector. Again, several more weeks before I could get another appointment.

Now you won't believe this, but it happened a third time on September 27, 1974. The two FAA chiefs got into a heated argument. The inspector had me fly him around the San Jose Airport traffic pattern once to a full stop, got out, and said, "Congratulations, you are now a flight instructor, and don't come back." It was probably the shortest check ride in the history of the FAA (15 min).

The irony of the story is that Greg, my roommate, was also working on his CFI certificate. When he went to the GADO several months later, they grilled him for nearly a full day and then required a flight of about 2 hours. He has never forgiven me.

The Christmas Card

Air traffic controllers are unique people, to say the least. Between Greg and another trainee, Ed Reed, and myself, we circulated the same Christmas card to each other for over 30 years by simply crossing out the last signature, re-signing and remailing. After all, it was the thought that counts.

The Gas Pumps

Directly across the runways from the control tower were the gas pumps where aircraft would refuel. When we were not preoccupied with aircraft in the flight pattern, we would watch the girls over there with the binoculars. Girl-watching was a favorite pastime. Noel who worked the fuel pit was our favorite.

Left to right: Gil Gonzales on his break, me working Local Control, and Greg Hildebrand working Ground Control at RHV.

Chapter 3

Sacramento Metro Airport (SMF), California

Mom

My mom, Katy, was diagnosed with terminal cancer. I arranged a hardship transfer to Sacramento with the help of Congressman Bizz Johnson in 1975. With Dad disabled and the two younger siblings still in high school, I was needed at home. Mom passed away just six weeks after the transfer at the age of 52. The Lord picks the prettiest flowers in his garden first.

I Didn't Say That!

Pacific Southwest Airlines (PSA) and Western Airlines (WA) would race gate to gate between Los Angeles and Sacramento. They had identical schedules. Approach Control handed PSA and WA off to me one day with WA on right downwind and PSA on left downwind with a smirk in his voice, "Metro, it's a tie; you call it." Great. He could have slowed one of the Boeings down a few minutes earlier.

Both came up on the frequency and someone said, "Say, ah, Metro Tower, we were first this morning . . . ah . . . Why don't you let PSA land first." I cleared PSA to land and sequenced WA number two to follow traffic turning base. There was a pause, and then the Western captain replied angrily that he didn't say that. The Western crew heard the laughter from the controllers in the background as I had to tell them again that he was still number two. PSA always had that "can do" attitude. Western pilots were conservative and flew like your grandmother.

Fog and the RVR

Metro Airport was built on the Sacramento River amongst the rice paddies and gets the worst fog in the valley. PSA needed 1200 feet Runway Visual Range (RVR) to launch, and if we didn't have the minimum visibility, they would taxi out anyway and wait in the run-up area hoping for a better weather report. This was a ruse. Several minutes later, they would call, ask for the RVR again, and if below legal takeoff minimums, ask to taxi back to the terminal via the runway.

We couldn't see them, but we could hear their engines. They would taxi abeam the RVR equipment along the runway which measured visibility, point their JT8D jet engines at the RVR, and run up the power. The hot air would dissipate the fog momentarily, and the RVR would jump to above takeoff minimums. With the improved visibility, we would clear them for takeoff, and they were on their way.

The other airlines in competition on the route didn't like being taken advantage of with this questionable procedure. They were losing customers and complained to the FAA Regional Office in Los Angeles. We were told that we couldn't give PSA takeoff clearance anymore under those conditions.

A Bunch of Cowboys

The PSA pilots would fly short approaches if asked to beat straight-in traffic several miles out on final. One captain would taxi to the gate with a 20-foot white silk scarf dangling from the side window and wearing an old WWI cloth helmet and goggles.

Before nosing into the gate opposite the large glass windows at the terminal, one captain would slide open his side window and put a rubber chicken on the outside of the front cockpit glass. The passengers would gather in large numbers to look down at the bird strike. On occasion, he would alternate with a "For Sale" sign in the cockpit window.

On another occasion, United Airlines was cleared for takeoff. After liftoff, they stated there was a dead rabbit on the runway. PSA was next for departure, and I asked them if they copied the UA transmission to which they replied: "Roger, we'll notify our caterers."

Cleared to Land

FAR 121.651 states in part that no pilot may land when the visibility is less than that required for the instrument approach which, for an ILS (Instrument Landing System), is 2,400 feet or 1,800 feet RVR depending on the runway. This is the same as 1/2 statute mile in prevailing visibility terms.

If a controller gives an arriving flight a lesser value before that flight arrives at the Outer Marker (OM) about 5 miles out, the flight cannot descend to minimums looking for the airport on the ILS.

We would defer adverse visibility reports to the crews until after they reported the OM, and then we cleared them to land, at which time they could descend to Decision Height (DH) of 200 feet Above Ground Level (AGL) looking for the approach lights or the runway and/or the airport.

Slant range visibility on final from the cockpit was different than the horizontal visibility observed along the runways with the RVR equipment (a laser transmitter and receiver) and different than what we could see from the tower cab situated some distance from the runways.

If the flight did a missed approach, it increased the controller workload. We would place the flight into a holding pattern some 1,000 feet above another airplane over the airport waiting for clearance to attempt another approach. I remember as many as eight aircraft on one occasion in the holding pattern due to fog. Each one had to be cleared to descend 1,000 feet as the previous aircraft reported out of his holding altitude. It was a lot of work, hence our enthusiasm to get them on the ground.

The Commute

It was 1977, and I would commute to work from a dirt strip in Loomis, CA in my little yellow biplane. Fritz and Claire Holsclaw owned the landing strip along the fence line of Interstate 80. My takeoffs and landings would sometimes stop traffic on Interstate 80 as it looked like I was landing on the freeway. The California Highway Patrol finally posted signs stating "No Stopping Allowed."

Flying to work above the road congestion below was a natural high. Dan Shively of Channel 3 KCRA-TV was doing traffic watch with a helicopter during these years and would occasionally ask me to do a flyby when he saw or heard me on the frequency over Sacramento when he needed to fill in a few seconds of TV time. I would rock my wings, do a 360-degree turn around him, fly by upside down, or do a roll as I went by.

Low Level Aerobatics

I walked into the FAA GADO at Sacramento Executive Airport and asked the inspector on front desk duty for an appointment to demonstrate my acrobatics skills for an aerobatics sign off. This would enable me to do low level aerobatics below 1,500 feet at air shows. His answer was, "No, we're too busy." That surprised me. Not only was I a fellow FAA employee, but a taxpayer who was requesting a service provided by the FAA.

I asked to see the facility chief, Bob Crass, who told me to sign myself off in my logbook. He said that since I was an FAA employee, he had no problem with that procedure. He watched me as I did it! You can't get away with this today.

The Union Flights Super Cub

Union Flights out of Sacramento Executive flew several con-tracts around the state for pipeline, power line, and water canal inspections. On this particular winter day, a cold front was blowing in off the Pacific, with winds picking up to 60 knots by midafternoon. Dave, in the Super Cub, normally flew from east to west through the control zone every day at the same time. It normally took the pilot about six minutes to transition through our airspace.

About 30 minutes later, Dave called over Woodland 10 miles west and asked to return back through. He was calling it quits only halfway through his route. The little Super Cub with 150 horses could not make any progress with those headwinds. To our surprise, he passed through by simple reducing power slightly and allowing the wind to carry him back tail first! We had never seen an aircraft flying backward.

Takeoff on the Ramp

The same afternoon, the winds were still gusting to 60 knots when I got off work. The winds were light when I flew to Sac Metro that morning in 25 minutes instead of driving 75 minutes. My little biplane was tied down on the ramp facing into the wind, but my rudder was not big enough to allow me to taxi to the runway with that crosswind.

I told my relief that I would call for taxi but not move out of my parking spot. Then five minutes later, I would call for takeoff as if I had taxied out to the runway. When cleared for takeoff, I would start my takeoff run directly into the wind and across the huge ramp in front of the terminal.

My first call to Ground Control went like this: "Good afternoon tower, N1PL request startup and push back," just like an airline captain. Then, cleared for takeoff a few minutes later, I was airborne in 100 feet. With a tailwind heading northeast, I was back at the landing strip in a record 10 minutes. Luckily, the dirt runway was directly aligned with the wind.

Night Approaches

PanAm and TWA would fly practice approaches all night with their Boeing 747s back in the seventies. This was before the proliferation of three-axis full-motion flight simulators. The tower was manned by one controller through the midnight shift, and it would take about 15 minutes between approaches. We would sometimes drift off into a light sleep, waiting for the next call on the frequency.

The controller, having a typical weekend off and then working on the backside of the clock that first evening, would have trouble staying awake. After several calls from the inbound traffic and no answer on the intercom from Sacramento Approach Control at McClellan Air Force Base, Felix, the overweight lineman from the fire station on the field was dispatched to the control tower. He ran up the stairs as fast as he could, only to find our buddy asleep in his chair. We were amazed that big old Felix didn't have a heart attack.

A Thousand Ways to Die

Dad asked me to fetch the morning paper for him. It was some 600 feet from the house to the road and too far for him to walk. One Sunday morning, I told him I would pick up the Sacramento Bee on the way to the strip about five miles away and would drop it to him as I flew over the house on the way to work. I was running late. It weighed as much as five pounds on Sunday.

I flew over the ranch at 200 feet and put the paper right on the doorstep. Dad heard me approaching and walked out the front door just as I dropped it. It nearly hit him. It probably would have gone through the roof if I had released a second later. Another brilliant idea that would have made the TV series, *A Thousand Ways to Die*.

Notices to Airmen on the FDEP Machine

Earlier, I mentioned the FDEP Machine used to pass IFR clearances and messages to appropriate stations along the route of flight. Here are a few of the NOTAMs that I saved over the years:

> BFL UA 061021 CESSNA ENTERED TEHACHAPI PASS WITH WINDOWS, EXITED WITHOUT. Translation: Bakersfield, Unidentified Aviator, sixth day of the month at 1021 Zulu time.

> SEA US 071525 80–100 MI W OF VANCOUVER ISLAND ON RTE TOKYO–SEATTLE. SEVERE TO EXTREME TURBULENCE. LOST 9000 FEET IN UNCONTROLLED DESCENT FROM FL390. BOEING KC135 TANKER.

> CMH US 011725 UNMANNED AIRCRAFT AERONCA CHAMP LAST SEEN HEADING NE FROM HAMILTON CO. AIRPORT AT 3000 FEET. (1997)

The pilot was hand-propping his aircraft due to a lack of an electrical system and had the throttle set wide open. The aircraft took off without him.

> SFO UA 080025 BAKERSFIELD, CA AREA. WINDSHIELD FULL OF BUGS. HARD TO SEE. 10000 FEET AND BELOW.

I wish I had saved the FDEP strip from the Mt. St. Helens eruption in 1978. I felt the tower shake slightly.

ATC Helps Out in Bank Heist

I had just relieved Tom McDonald at local control as his shift ended at 2 p.m. when I noticed the commotion down at the terminal. Lots of cops. Someone had just robbed Bank of America, and they were looking for the suspect. Activity went on all afternoon and spread to the adjoining cornfields on the airport.

The next day, we were still discussing it when the supervisor, John Foster, brought up a composite drawing. Tom fell out of his chair. He had picked up the guy hitchhiking on his way out of the airport and didn't know the bank had been robbed until he came to work the next day. Said he was a very nice gentleman, and they exchanged pleasantries all the way to Woodland, some ten miles west of the airport.

What's Your Position?

Working the early morning rush at Sacramento Metro one morning, the first inbound was United from San Francisco and connecting on to Denver. Approach Control (radar) handed United off to me early about 40 miles out as he had no other traffic.

United finally called, and as I had some departures to launch, I needed to know exactly where he was. I asked him to state his position, and he said he was the copilot. "Would I like to talk to the Captain?" The captain was circling his house and vineyards in Napa to impress his first officer.

The NDB Approach

It was one of those foggy, gray winter days in Sacramento. A Boeing 747 was doing practice Nondirectional Beacon (nonprecision) approaches to Runway 34. The tower at Metro is at least a quarter mile to the side of the runway.

Bob Markwith, the Chief, was on local control when the 747 popped out of the low undercast headed directly for and level with the tower cab at 150 feet. I've never seen an old man move so fast.

He beat all of us kids down the stairs as the 747 roared over the top of us and back up into the clouds.

Bob continued down to his office to call Approach Control to inform the pilots they were no longer welcome at Metro. He never did come back upstairs that day.

John Foster

John was our supervisor and a great manager. He was well-liked by all the controllers. Years later, after he retired, I bumped into him at Home Depot and discovered he was working for an insurance company and not happy. I had bought Airline Ground Schools (AGS) in 1987 and asked John if he would like to manage it for me. He accepted and did a wonderful job. I would tease him about getting even. It was my turn to be the boss.

The Pool Table

My family had a drive-in restaurant, the Suzy Q, and across the street: a pool hall in Fair Oaks, CA; a suburb of Sacramento. We had a surplus pool table, and on the bottom floor of the control tower, we had an empty room. We didn't have a break room like most control towers, and I suggested to the chief that we install the pool table. He agreed, and it was the only FAA facility in the country with a pool table instead of a TV room.

Hughes Air West

In 1976, before Hughes Air West merged with Republic, one of their yellow DC9 airliners would depart around 10:30 each night to Klamath Falls, OR. After pushback, they would pass the terminal on their way to the runway and someone on the airport would key a microphone to the sound of a long, lonesome train whistle passing through a railroad crossing.

Traffic Count Record

October 7, 1975, while working light traffic and chitchatting with my fellow controllers, the conversation drifted around to a favorite topic: how controllers got paid. It was based on the traffic count. Sac Metro was a GS-10 tower. Sac Exec was a GS-11 tower because they had more traffic. Each takeoff and landing was counted and tallied toward an annual figure.

I had a bright idea that could raise our traffic count at Metro. At lunch, I could fly my little biplane up and down the runway doing touch-and-go's. Each controller could chip in a few bucks for gas. At the time, the highest hourly traffic count had been 40. Cleared for takeoff, I was airborne in 400 feet, climbed to 50 feet above the ground, and then requested landing. I was able to do six takeoffs and landings (total count 12) in just one pass down the 8,000 foot runway. I then reversed course at the far end and repeated the sequence going the opposite direction; another 12 count for a total of 24.

With the 20 commercial operations interrupting my routine, we achieved a record 126 count in one hour. The only problem was the controllers didn't want to pay for the gas. Metro made Level 11 several years later.

Pilot Controller Exchanges

A PanAm B747 requested his clearance back home one morning after training all night with us. I replied, "And where is the worlds' most experienced airline going this morning without filing a flight plan?" His dispatch office had dropped the ball. We typed it into the computer for him.

A Cessna 150 put-put called and asked, "You sure you want me to taxi in front of the 747?" My response: "Ya, he's not hungry."

Familiarization Flights

The FAA has a policy allowing controllers to ride along in the cockpit with the air carriers to get a better picture of the cockpit workload. Pilots were also encouraged to visit us in the tower. We were allowed seven familiarization flights a year, but each one had to be on a different air carrier.

PSA had an unofficial policy of ignoring the FAA rule. We could ride with them as many times as we wished. Our tower chief was on a fam flight one morning, and we conspired to have a little fun at his expense.

Just after takeoff, we would instruct the pilots to contact Departure Control. I asked the radar controller to change the phraseology and say, "For radar identification, throw your jumpseater out the window!" The chief never found out we were the instigators.

PSA Flight 182, San Diego (SAN), September 15, 1978

I was working ground control at 10:30 p.m. the night before the accident. A PSA B727 arrived from Los Angeles and taxied to the gate. One of the pilots invited me to a party at the Host Hotel between the tower and the terminal. I declined. I had a short eight-hour turnaround and had to be back to work the next morning at 7 a.m., my last day of the week.

As I drove onto the airport the next morning, I saw PSA taking off for Los Angeles and then on to SAN. The controller I relieved told me that he could see the crew having a good time at the pool all night long from our high vantage point.

Inbound to SAN on a visual approach on a sunny day, PSA was given traffic, a Cessna 172 ahead and below their flight path. The crew stated they had the traffic in sight but lost sight of the Cessna amongst the multicolored rooftops below. A midair collision occurred. There were no survivors: 144 on board plus seven civilians on the ground.

This was the deadliest crash in the United States to date. ATC had a conflict alert 19 seconds before impact, but the controller did not feel a call to PSA was necessary as the crew had stated they had the Cessna in sight.

Fatigue had to have been a factor, as the crew did not get much sleep the night before. The NTSB report did not mention the party as a contributing factor and probably did not know about it.

We have a term, Tombstone Technology, to describe improvements to the system when we have a preventable accident. The three-man crew plus two jumpseating pilots in the cockpit were talking about personal matters. We now have a regulation: FAR Part 121.542, Flight Crewmember Duties, that states, "No idle chitchat below 10,000 feet." It is commonly referred to as the "sterile cockpit rule."

Chapter 4

Sacramento Executive Airport (SAC), California

I bid Sac Exec and was awarded a slot. It was the original airport in Sacramento, but the runways were too short for large jets. The tower was atop the terminal with a Red Baron Restaurant below. All the flight schools were within a city block. SAC was a popular refueling stop for north–south traffic between Seattle and San Diego. Due to itinerant traffic and lots of flight training, it was a GS-11 tower.

The PIREP

It was a cold, rainy day. We were sitting around the tower cab, engaged in one of the usual intellectual discussions, when a weak call came in with inexperience written all over it. I replied on the frequency expecting the worse; a student pilot trapped in deteriorating weather.

Communication was bad, and I asked his call sign several times. He wanted to file a PIREP (Pilot Report). "Okay, go ahead."

"It's raining on the ramp." "What?" "It's raining on the ramp." "Where are you?" "I'm parked below the control tower."

The student pilot had been told to report any weather he encountered. He had done his preflight inspection and, while sitting in the C150 waiting for the instructor, did exactly as he had been told in ground school. Without the engine running, the weak battery was powering the radio, and it sounded like he was miles away.

An interesting fact about Californian weather: when the central valley fogged in, the foothill airports along the Sierra Mountains to the east would be open and vice versa.

The Preflight Inspection

Flight instructors would send their students out to the flight line to inspect the aircraft before flight. One of their popular tricks (a teaching moment) was to throw a few nuts and bolts under the aircraft before the student arrived at the aircraft. When the instructor finally came out to the aircraft, he would ask the student about the hardware lying on the ground and inform him the aircraft was not airworthy. This took place directly below the tower and was fun to watch the faces of the students when they realized they had missed something very important.

Another popular hazing moment occurred when an instructor would inform a student that he needed a bucket of prop wash and send the student to the maintenance shop to fetch it. There is no such thing.

Five Weeks below Landing Minimums

One winter, Sac Exec was below landing minimums (200 foot ceilings and visibility less than 1/2 SM) for over five weeks straight. You could takeoff under Federal Aviation Regulations Part 91 with no visibility on an IFR flight plan but could not land. I took off one morning with a rented Cessna 172 by following the painted white centerline on the runway.

Just after liftoff, a big thump was heard. A quick scan at the instrument panel showed no discrepancies, and the only thing to do was to continue climbing to sunshine on top of the valley fog. Once there at 2,000 feet, it was obvious what the problem was: a large dent in the left wing with telltale white feathers and some blood. Seagulls sit on runways in low visibility conditions, and the county had not swept the runway with a pickup truck before our departure as required.

Free Gas!

The line service fellas were required to drain five gallons of fuel from each storage tank in the mornings to make sure there was no water condensation contaminating the fuel. They were not allowed to pour it back into the tanks but had to dispose of it. Normally, they would save it for practice fire drills. When I discovered this, I mentioned to them that if it looked good, they could just pour it into my airplane on the ramp. Got lots of free fuel and repaid them with pizzas, beer, and donuts from time to time.

The GI Bill

While working at Executive, I took advantage of the GI Bill and finished acquiring all of my pilot certificates, including the multiengine ATP (Airline Transport Pilot) in an old Piper Apache. You lose an engine on that twin, and the other engine would carry you to the scene of the accident.

One in a Hundred

In late 1978, my tower chief talked me into bidding on a radar position at Edwards Air Force Base (AFB) with the lure of more money (GS-12). It was time to move up to a busier facility. The traffic level at SAC was no longer challenging. The kids were older now and able to help with dad.

The FAA has stated that only one in a hundred prospects have what is required to be selected and to complete the training as an air traffic controller. The job is considered one of the most mentally challenging careers and is notoriously stressful based on a number of variables involving equipment, configuration, weather, traffic volume, human factors, management, etc.

Controllers are well-organized, quick with numbers, have assertive and firm decision-making skills, can maintain composure under pressure, and have excellent short-term memories. Numerous studies show them with an excellent visual memory and high degree of situational awareness significantly better than the average population. In experiments involving short-term memory, peer-induced stress, and real-time risk analysis, controllers scored better than the control group every time. Wikipedia

It was an honor to have been selected, and a challenge to multitask numerous aircraft with hundreds of lives depending on me for the safe and expeditious movement of traffic. I take great satisfaction for a job well-done in my eight years as an air traffic controller. I never left anybody up there.

Chapter 5

Edwards Approach Control (EDW), Edwards AFB, California

The FAA radar facility was located on a hill overlooking Edwards AFB. The primary mission was to support the Air Force activities in the restricted airspace surrounding the base and the activities at Groom Lake (Area 51). The  Air Force had the ability to look at their test pilots in the cockpit from the Range Office at Edwards. The cameras could watch the flights two hundred miles out. The photographic detail was incredible.

The Midnight Shift

The journeymen controllers would play poker all night in the center of the radar room while we rookies would work the radar scopes. Our radar had a range out to 200 miles. We covered the area from the Colorado River to the east and to the west, the Tehachapi Mountains. To the north, Bishop, CA and to the San Gabriel Mountains to the south.

Requesting Flight Level 600

We had a SR71 Blackbird request FL 600 (60,000 ft). The airspace at that time only went up to Flight Level 450. The controller laughed and said to the pilot, "If you can get up to 600, you can have it" to which the pilot replied, "No, you don't understand. I want to come down to FL600." The pilot was just trying to be funny.

Lost Aircraft

I overheard a busy controller sitting at the next scope respond to an aircraft reporting that he was lost. "Lost aircraft calling Edwards Approach, say your position." The busy journeyman controller never lived that one down.

We Got a Deal

Emergencies were common at Edwards with all the test flights. The radar room was on the second floor, and we had a door that opened to the roof overlooking the runway. If we had an emergency inbound (a deal), the controller working the aircraft would inform the supervisor and people on a break would scramble to the roof to watch the excitement. I saw several crashes on the runway.

The Mother Ship

Edwards had one KC-135 tanker (Boeing 707) assigned to it for its refueling missions. When they first acquired it, the Air Force was unaware that there was a nonstandard 10,000 pound fuel tank up forward. On one of the first missions, the refuelers were told to top off the fuel tanks. They found the extra tank. On takeoff, the pilots used most of the 14,000 foot dry lake bed to get airborne because they were nose heavy. They barely cleared the power lines on the highway some five miles northeast of the complex. They should have aborted the takeoff.

Don't Mess With a Marine

We heard a story from Los Angeles Center about a Marine Corps Harrier Jump Jet on an Instrument Flight Plan on the V12 airway who experienced a near midair with another aircraft while under their control. The marine pilot was so angry with ATC that he canceled IFR and proceeded directly to the Los Angeles Center parking lot in Palmdale where he landed vertically. He calmly walked into the Center demanding to see the controller who nearly killed him. Upon being introduced, he punched him in the face, and then walked back out to his waiting jet, departing just as he had arrived.

You gotta admire how the Marines solve their problems, and you can bet the controller always gave excellent service to the Marine pilots after that. Hey folks, I wouldn't lie to you. The truth is stranger than fiction.

Home for the Weekend

I would fly home to Loomis on my days off. I could make it in three hours in my Piper Pacer which I obtained by trading the Smith Miniplane or it would take 2.4 hours in the Mong biplane which I had built. The Mong had a shorter range, so I installed an extra tank to hold a little more fuel. At two hours, the engine would begin to sputter, and I would select the auxiliary tank and hit the manual wobble pump to keep it running while diving to keep the prop from stopping. I didn't have an electrical system. That gave me the ability to make the last 24 minutes nonstop with a 25 minute reserve on landing.

Piper Pacer

Mong Biplane

On August 7, 1978, I borrowed a no-radio Taylorcraft from Joe Williams to fly to work from the Rio Linda Airport in Sacramento while my aircraft was in the shop for an annual inspection. Arriving at Mojave about 3 a.m. after a 3.5 hour flight, I discovered the winds were gusting to 60 mph below on the airport and kicking up quite a bit of sand and dust.

If I landed on the runway, I wouldn't be able to turn 90 degrees onto the taxiway—not enough rudder to counter the wind, plus the wind would probably flip the aircraft over. My only choice was to land directly into the wind over the tiedown spot on the ramp. My forward speed matched the headwind, and I simply flew the aircraft as if in a hover, down to a landing.

The next problem after shutting down the engine was that I could not get out of the aircraft without it blowing away. As long as I sat in the cockpit and held the brakes, and the elevator and aileron controls to offset the wind, I was rocking a lot, but ok.

I had to wait until the gas boy showed at 7 a.m. to help me secure the bird. He parked the fuel truck in front of me to block the wind and chocked and tied down the airplane allowing me to exit. I often wondered if I could log the four hours I flew the aircraft without the engine running while sitting on the ramp.

Big Sky, Little Bullet

Highway 58 runs east–west between Mojave and Barstow and skirts the north boundary of Edwards AFB. Overlying the highway is Restricted Airspace R-2515. There is a FAA Letter of Agreement (LOA) with the local pilots allowing transition along the road below 400 feet AGL (Above Ground Level) even when the Restricted Area is hot. The locals are the Borax Plant, the California Highway Patrol, local ranchers, and the power line patrol Super Cub from Union Flights.

I flew the route in my no-radio Mong biplane several times. No communications are required from the locals by Letter of Agreement with the FAA. Now I wasn't a signature to that document, but on the radar scope, you couldn't tell who was and who wasn't. I simply took advantage of the system. I looked like a truck on the highway on the radar scope.

I would fly to Needles, AZ on the Colorado River to listen to the ASU football games on Saturday nights on my portable AM radio. The "Big Sky, Little Bullet" theory worked every time. With no electrical system, I would fly back with just a flashlight to check my instrument panel. When the sun went down, the officers club became very busy, and there was never any traffic out there over the high desert. I had become a rogue pilot who followed the rules only when it suited me.

31 Flavors

The highlight of the afternoons was the ice cream run to the 31 Flavors shop on base. A trainee would be volunteered to collect the money and the orders from the journeyman controllers and then fetch some 30–40 pints of ice cream in several large coolers packed with ice. It could easily top 100+ degrees in the summer on the high desert.

Top Secret

Whenever some exotic new design flew into Edwards and landed from Area 51, the Air Force would shut down their control tower and take their enlisted personnel downstairs to a secure room where they could not see the aircraft. They didn't know that we had access to the roof of our facility and could see everything. The flight strip with the call sign lacking the aircraft type was an indication something interesting was about to arrive. I got to see several unusual aircraft before the general public or Aviation Week (Leak) and Space Technology published anything.

The Trainee

I was working my sector with the old TPX-42 WWII black and white radar scope, and the instructor at the next radar console was working with his trainee. She had four Lockheed USAF C130 Hercs doing practice approaches at the Air Force Plant 42 in her sector plus a civilian twin, a Cessna 310 mixed in among them. Civilians can do practice approaches to a military installation but cannot land.

Also inbound from Miramar Naval Air Station near San Diego were about 30 fighters for the annual Operation Red Flag in our restricted airspace. Normally, they would be handed off to us by Los Angeles Center as flights of two or four. For some unknown reason, they were all single ship operations this time.

A journeyman controller would be hard-pressed to handle this influx of aircraft all within a few minutes. Our trainee was about to go down the tubes. Her frequency was overloaded with calls for permission to enter the airspace.

The Cessna was on a vector to intercept the ILS at Plant 42, and she was not able to give him instructions to turn inbound due to frequency congestion. He passed through the ILS on a 90 degree angle. She shortly managed to turn him outbound away from the airport to parallel the ILS localizer. At the appropriate moment, she turned him inbound again on a base entry to intercept the localizer and was then jumped by several more fighters on the frequency. Back through the ILS again went the twin Cessna.

The trainee was getting frustrated and her instructor, standing behind her, had this big smile on his face. He pointed at the Cessna target on the radar screen indicting she needed to do something with him. Once more, she turned him outbound to parallel the inbound course. He was halfway to George AFB to the east by now.

Finally, in desperation, she lost the big picture and, in nonstandard phraseology, said to the Cessna, November 43 Bravo, "Take over visually and save yourself." The instructor took over the position but never did live down the laughter from his fellow controllers who overheard everything.

Cheryl and Pacific Gas and Electric (PG&E)

The closest civilian airport to Edwards AFB was Mojave, California where I purchased a 60-foot mobile home and based my airplane. I would commute home to Northern California from the high desert on my weekends. There was absolutely nothing to do in the little railroad town of Mojave on my days off.

On the morning of my weekly trip to Southern California, Dad and I drove the five miles to my hangar at the strip in Loomis. Driving in on the dirt road, we were passed by a PG&E pickup truck traveling fast in the opposite direction in a big cloud of dust. We only got a glimpse of the female meter reader. To get a laugh out of Dad, I went to the meter at the back of the hangar and wrote in grease pencil, "Meter Reader, would you like to go for a ride in my airplane?"

She only read the meter once a month, and it was about two months later, as I lay under my airplane in the hangar cleaning the fuselage, that I learned she had replied. Claire Holsclaw, who owned the flight strip with her husband, Fritz, had stopped to water her horse at the back of the hangar and saw the message. She came into the hangar laughing and asked about the meter reader. All it said was "Okay." No name or phone number. I erased and started again, "What's your name and phone number?"

She replied on her next visit with "Cheryl" and an Auburn phone number about 10 miles up the road.

I forgot about it again. Several more months passed when in late December. Dad came by on his way to the Loomis Dairy Queen to get a cheeseburger. I had not had lunch so he picked up a hamburger for me too. It was 4 o'clock when he returned, and he thought about the meter box.

It was Christmas, and I called the number. Not knowing what to say, I asked Cheryl if she would like to go to dinner, having just eaten a late lunch. She agreed cautiously, and I rushed home to shower and change. Arriving at 6 p.m., we discovered that neither of us were really hungry and all the restaurants were now closed. We got ice cream. She was absolutely gorgeous!

The Emergency

I invited Cheryl to ride along in the back of my Piper Pacer while I gave Greg Toste a flight lesson the next day. As the flight progressed, I completely forgot she was in the back, and pulled the power off and told Greg he had just lost the engine. As we descended and Greg searched for a suitable emergency landing site, Cheryl thought it was a real emergency but didn't say a word. At about 500 feet, I pushed the throttle in and told Greg that the field over the left would have been a better place to land. We climbed back to altitude and completed the flight lesson.

After landing back in Loomis, Cheryl expressed her concern that we were going to crash. I was apologetic. It never occurred to me to brief her on what I was doing. In spite of this, she agreed to see me again the next weekend. Two weeks later, I proposed to her, and two years later, she accepted.

Greg Toste passed his private pilot checkride in the Piper Pacer. I told him if he got close to his destination with the FAA inspector and didn't see the airport, say, "I see the airport," and watch to see which direction the inspector looked. It is a natural response. Then turn in that direction. Greg eventually bought the airplane from me. He still has it.

Flight Instructor Rules

I had several rules as a flight instructor which were published in the Pacific Flyer newspaper.

1. The instructor always makes the rules. No student could possibly know all the rules.
2. The rules are subject to change at any time without prior notification.
3. If the instructor suspects the student knows all the rules, he must immediately change some or all of the rules.
4. The instructor is never wrong.
5. If the instructor is wrong, it is because of a flagrant misunderstanding which was the direct result of something the student did or said.
6. If rule 5 applies, the student must immediately apologize for causing the misunderstanding.
7. The instructor can change his mind at any time.
8. The student is not allowed to change his mind without express written consent of the instructor.
9. The instructor has the right to be angry at any time.
10. The student must remain calm at all times unless the instructor wants him to be angry or upset.

September 5, 1980, Marriage

I called Stan Brown, an attorney and friend in Reno, and told him on a Friday afternoon that Cheryl and I were eloping and would be there in about two hours. Stan and I raced biplanes together. He was married to a beautiful blond, Elaine, a former American Airlines flight attendant. He said he would take care of all the arrangements. He and Elaine were our best man and woman at the ceremony. The entire weekend was complimentary: hotel, meals, shows, the works.

Stanley was an institution in Reno and had all the connections. He was the attorney for Joe Comforte who owned the Mustang Ranch (aka brothel) east of Reno. When I tell local folks who knew

Stanley that he was our best man, they always wonder if I met Cheryl at the Mustang.

Smoke

Most controllers smoked, and Edwards RAPCON was no different. The smoke was so stifling that I could not wear my contacts. At times, you couldn't see across the radar room.

I had to get out of that place. The other consideration was that there was no classroom training for new radar controllers. You were immediately put on a radar scope with a journeyman controller and taught according to his ability as an impromptu instructor. This lead to nonstandardization among the controllers. Good people with good intentions but less than ideal results.

I bid on an opening at Bakersfield Tower and Manual Approach Control and was selected.

Chapter 6

Bakersfield Meadows Airport (BFL), California

I was back in the central valley. No more flying the Tehachapi Mountains from Sacramento to Mojave in the dark to get back to work on my Monday mornings at Edwards. This shortened my commute to Sacramento by 30 minutes.

The tower controllers would watch for me starting about 15 minutes before I was due to report to work at BFL tower after my weekend if I was flying the Mong. I didn't have a radio and would rely on them to give me a green light indicating I was cleared to land. On several occasions they would forget me, and I would have to circle to the west of the airport for 10–15 minutes before someone would realize I was late for work. They would then pick up the binoculars to see if I was in the area. The Mong had a 15 foot wingspan and it was hard to see me.

UNO

Things would get really slow at night in BFL, and we would play UNO for soda pops to pass the time. We'd all stand around the supervisor desk in the center of the tower cab with our headsets on while playing cards and wait for someone to call.

When I left BFL for Stockton Tower and Approach Control, the supervisor, Kenny Knoben (affectionately known as Obi-wan Kenobi), owed me over 90 cokes. Until he retired, I would say "UNO" in the blind whenever I overflew BFL to remind him how bad he was at cards. I understand he never did figure out how to play the game. I guess that's why they promoted him to management.

The Clock

We were sitting around the break room about 10 minutes before the end of the shift. The tower chief walked in and asked us to move a filing cabinet which was blocking the view of the clock on the wall.

Kenny began to complain rather loudly that he couldn't see the clock from where he was sitting. I suggested he look at his watch to which he replied, "What, are you nuts? Look at MY watch on government time." Spoken like a real manager.

Foreign Students

IASCO, a flight school in Napa, CA, did a lot of ab initio pilot training for foreign airlines including Japan Airlines and Korean Air. Their students on cross-country flights would show up in the traffic patterns at all the airports in California. Unfortunately, they were usually going the wrong direction—directly into the face of oncoming traffic in spite of very precise instructions from the controllers.

We would speak slowly for them since English was a second language, and their comprehension was not good. The local flight instructors in the pattern with students would either land or depart the pattern when they heard these guys call for landing instructions. Every pair of eyeballs in the tower including the controllers on break would pick up the binoculars and start scanning all directions for our Kamikaze pilots. We would hear things like: "Tower, please speak slowly. I am a baby in English and lonely in the cockpit."

Taildragger Checkout

Several of us in the control tower were pilots, but Walter "Red" Ray had not flown a taildragger. One slow afternoon, June 4, 1979, Ken Knoben suggested I take my fellow controllers for a familiarization ride around the Bakersfield Meadows Airport. As expected, Red was all over the runway trying to control my PA20 Piper Pacer, N5926D.

On the last landing, we actually departed the runway off the left into the grass between the parallel runways, and Al Dilger, the controller, asked us on the air, "26D, do you need any assistance or would you just like a little music?"

Following the PATCO (controller) strike in 1981, Red was hired by Skywest Airlines. Sadly, he was the first officer on a flight involved in a midair with a Mooney over Salt Lake City Airport #2 in 1987. There were no survivors. He left behind a wife and six kids. Red was a good man.

1979 - The Subpoena

Jimmy Miller, a Formula One race pilot, was putting on a July air race in his hometown of San Marcos, Texas. I asked the supervisor for a few days vacation. He said, "No, we're short-staffed."

A few days later, Stan Brown in Reno called to tell me the rendezvous point was Barstow as we always traveled east in a loose ship formation of four to five biplanes for the races. I said I couldn't go.

A week later, the Tower Chief received a subpoena in the mail instructing me to report to Reno for a T6 air race accident investigation the same day everyone was leaving for Texas. I called Stan, and he said the deposition had been moved to San Marcos, TX. I departed RHV headed north for Reno and, as soon as I was out of sight, changed course to the southeast for the high desert and the Barstow rendezvous.

I had to fly 1700 miles so Stanley could take my statement as a member of the United States Air Racing Association Board. Upon arrival in San Marcos, he asked me what I knew about the T6 midair at Reno Stead, and I told him I didn't see it. Took third in the Gold Race. On the way home, I realized the trade papers would carry the results and, for several months thereafter, made a point to dispose of any aviation magazines in the break room which might incriminate me.

Nick Gallmeister

Nick was one of my flight students at Reid-Hillview who eventually landed a job flying a Beech Queen Air for a corporation in Bakersfield at the same time I was working there. We had met at the Greek Orthodox Church in San Jose. Another gifted pilot and a good friend.

He eventually moved on to the airlines with a first officer position at Wisconsin Air. It's another sad story. In 1980, he was flying right seat on the Swearingen Metroliner (flight 965) that crashed in a thunderstorm on approach into Omaha, Nebraska.

The Center Weather Service Unit meteorologists failed to disseminate critical weather information to Omaha Approach Control supervisors that there was a Level Five thunderstorm east of the city. Before the supervisor could tell the sector controller about it, Air Wisconsin had entered the storm.

They flamed out both engines on the twin-engine Metroliner from water ingestion and were caught in a microburst (downdraft) and impacted in a corn field with only 2 survivors out of 13 souls on board.

I received a letter from Nick just three weeks earlier saying that he had died and gone to heaven, having now achieved a lifelong goal of flying for an airline.

Bryan Allen

Bryan was a cyclist and hang glider enthusiast who piloted the Gossamer Condor human-powered aircraft in 1977 for designer, Paul MacCready. Together, they won the Kremer Prize for a "first" in aviation for flying across the English Channel.

Several years later, Bryan was on his student cross-country flight, preparing for his private pilot certificate while I was working local control at BFL. He asked on the frequency if there was someone in the tower who could sign his logbook certifying he had completed that leg of his flight. I told him it would be an honor to do that for him, and I signed him off.

The Goodyear Blimp

Goodyear would give rides to their dealers around the country. They would also extend the courtesy to controllers. I got the ride in Columbia on October 2, 1979 and became a member of the Goodyear Blimp Club. I've got the card to prove it.

Chapter 7

Stockton Metro Airport (SCK), California

I got a transfer to Stockton Approach Control and Tower to be closer to home in Newcastle. California. SCK was a combined manual approach control/tower just like Bakersfield. Radar was being installed but not yet operational. It was a one hour 40 minute drive but on a good day, only 40 minutes by air. I wasn't there long enough to get into mischief before we went on strike.

Professional Air Traffic Controller Organization (PATCO) Strike

It was during this time that PATCO decided to strike. There were a number of issues on the table and pay was one of them, but not the main issue as told by the press. I was making $25,486 a year with eight years of service. That was a lot of money for a single guy. Today, the entry level salary is $36,559 and tops out at $152,521. The average pay for controllers is $80,938.

Our inability to work with the bureaucratic and overbearing management, plus safety, antiquated equipment, fatigue, workload, and the need for reduced working hours were the primary concerns. I recall something like 108 items on the negotiating table of which we expected to lose about half of these.

Controllers in other countries worked fewer hours per week due to the stress. In Austria and Belgium, they worked 35 hours; Canada and Denmark, 34 hours; Euro-Control, 29 hours; New Zealand, 32 hours; and West Germany, 33 hours per week. 89 percent of the U.S. controllers who retired between 1976 and 1979 did so due to medical issues (stress) before reaching retirement age.

I was at strike headquarters in Sacramento the night when the vote was taken. There were several hundred controllers present from around Northern California. The union stewards did not take a vote but just a head count and called that number in to union headquarters in support of the strike. Interesting concept.

The PATCO union had been taken over by a small group of radicals who lead 11,000 controllers down the road to destruction. It was August and summer vacation for America. The interruption in service was an inconvenience and could have been better served at another time of the year.

Robert Poli, President of PATCO, had provided the membership with a letter from Ronald Reagan dated October 20, 1980 in support of the air traffic controllers. In exchange, PATCO endorsed Reagan for president. A few weeks following our strike of August 3, 1981, the US Postal Service was facing a strike with their personnel, and the president could not afford to let them strike. In a change of heart, his only option was to order us back to work.

I had taken a week of vacation and was at home when the strike happened. The FAA reportedly called each controller and told them to report back to work. I was in a different area code. They did not call me, and they couldn't show any phone company documentation that they had phoned me. Nevertheless, I supported the strike and did not return. My eight year career was over.

There were reports of suicides and bankruptcies over the next few years. Unfortunate, but two years earlier, we had gone through the same stonewalling by the FAA on contract negotiations. The union told everyone to start saving their money in case the next go-around resulted in a strike. Many did not.

A lot of ATC management types who did not have the required second class medical certificates were found to be miraculously healthy and began handling traffic along with some military controllers loaned to the FAA. The system was able to cope without us. It was a major miscalculation.

You would think the FAA would reorganize management or correct their internal procedures on dealing with the rank and file. No, those who do not remember the past are condemned to repeat it. Having destroyed PATCO, another union was created five years later due to mismanagement and the same problems as before.

A third and final report on the ATC system was issued following the strike and concluded the FAA had developed "a rigid and insensitive system of people management" and morale problems experienced in the past are "reasserting themselves." The report of an independent task force created by Transportation Secretary Drew Lewis noted, "Unless it wants a repetition of the events of 1981, it will have to drastically change its management style."

The report stated that FAA supervisors were "autocratic; the FAA was guilty of heavy-handed supervision, and the agency seems headed toward more people-related problems in the future" Flightline Times, March 24, 1982.

I was one of the fortunate ones. I had some savings, and a job offer to fly a Cessna Citation jet for the AMSOIL Corporation in Superior, Wisconsin.

Years later, while living in Reno, I saw a newspaper article announcing that the PATCO controllers were finally allowed to apply for reinstatement. I called the FAA Western Region in Los Angeles and was told that they had sent a letter to my old address and it had been returned to them as undeliverable.

I asked why they didn't check their database for a current address since I was a pilot and my records were current. They couldn't answer my question. The deadline had expired for reinstatement. Oh well, I was gainfully employed as president and owner of Bill Phelps' Airline Ground Schools (AGS) at the time and doing very well.

The PATCO strike was the first sign of a decline of organized labor nationwide. The failure of ALPA (Air line Pilots Association) to support the controllers was a big disappointment to many of us.

Chapter 8

AMSOIL Synthetic Lubricants, Superior, Wisconsin

AMSOIL is a pioneer synthetic lubricants company and operated a Cessna Citation jet, serial number 6, based at Duluth, MN across the river from the company headquarters in Superior, WI. The founder and president, Al Amatuzio, was a former fighter pilot who recognized the superiority of synthetic oil in jet engines and saw the advantages for providing it to the automobile market.

I had become a part-time dealer of the products in California several years earlier. While I was building a new, synthetic (carbon fiber and fiberglass) race plane for the National Championship Air Races, AMSOIL became interested in the project. It would be a new synthetic airplane with a new synthetic aviation oil. It was a match made in heaven for an advertising executive.

AVOIL

AMSOIL was also developing a synthetic AVOIL for the piston-engine aircraft market. In 1981, Al Amatuzio offered to fund the new aircraft but on one condition that the company would own the airplane. I would be the pilot of record for world speed record attempts, air races, and promotional tours. I accepted. After the PATCO strike in August, I was offered a full-time position in Superior, Wisconsin and assigned to the Technical Services Department which included flying right seat on the company jet.

Al Unser Junior and Bobby Unser

One of my collateral duties was coaching young Al Unser Jr. (age 16) in public speaking—the number one fear of most people. Al Jr. was a budding race car driver like his dad, Al Sr. His uncle, Bobby Unser had used the AMSOIL 20W-50 Racing Oil in his Indy cars and became a spokesman for AMSOIL. It was not an approved lubricant at the Indy 500 so Bobby would sneak it into the Indy garage in milk cartons.

On November 4, 1983, I was the copilot on the Citation from St. Paul, Minnesota to Wichita, Kansas with Al Amatuzio and Bobby Unser in the back. On arrival, I got the keys for the rental car. Bobby took the keys from me and drove us to the AMSOIL meeting. He was doing 100 mph in downtown Wichita and scared the hell out of me sitting in the front seat with Al in the backseat laughing at me while I was hanging on with both hands.

Dad, Bobby Unser, and me

Al Amatuzio

Let me tell you about Al Amatuzio, the consummate entre-preneur. He became my role model for my business adventures in the years to follow. Today, we have great business people like Mick Romney and Donald Trump, and Al stands tall amongst them.

Al had both leadership and management qualities which we Americans admire. Some people are leaders, and some are managers. To find both traits in one individual is unique. His staff loved him, and they were motivated. He built AMSOIL into the leader in the field of synthetic lubrication recognized by all the major oil compa-nies. It was a pleasure to work for him.

In 1984, the company decided to sell the old company jet, and I wanted to fly. It was time to move on. I took a position in Southern California teaching weekend ground schools for Bill Phelps' Airline Ground Schools with an eye on the airlines. To this day, I remain a staunch AMSOIL supporter and use the products in my vehicles.

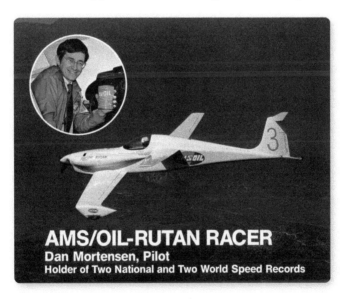

AMS/OIL-RUTAN RACER
Dan Mortensen, Pilot
Holder of Two National and Two World Speed Records

Chapter 9

Closed Course Pylon Air Racing

My air racing career continued after leaving AMSOIL. I was originally inspired by a photo of Don Fairbanks of Cincinnati in a Knight Twister biplane on the cover of Homebuilt Aircraft in the 1970s. Looking back through my logbooks, here is how it all started . . .

June 28, 1975, Beckwourth Airport, California

While barnstorming through the Sierra Nevada Mountains one beautiful afternoon in my open-cockpit Smith Miniplane, I landed at Beckwourth Airport for fuel. Frank Nervino was doing an annual inspection on the Sorceress, a one of a kind, all-metal negative-stagger biplane built for racing. The owner, Don Beck, was present and invited me to go biplane racing at the Lincoln, California air show near Sacramento the following May.

He mentioned a trophy and a hotel room. I told him I lived a few miles from there and didn't need a hotel room but was intrigued.

 Then he pointed out that I could use the airplane to make money as an advertising tool and write off the expenses on income tax. That got my interest.

May 16, 1976, My First Air Race

I was the slowest competitor out of five ships at Lincoln. I did not finish the race (DNF). Everyone had landed and I was still on the 3.1 mile course, so rather than hold up the air show, I landed. I realized in the race that I was being lapped at a blistering speed 119.76 mph and started cutting pylons (13 of them) in an attempt to keep up with the others.

I was trying to fly a shorter course to no avail. The course had a one-mile straight-away with a 180 degree turn at both ends with three pylons on each end. These were 35 foot towers with a red and white 55 gallon drum located on top. The home pylon at midfield in front of the crowd was the starting and ending point where the timers were located. I would turn inside of pylon 2 and skip 3 and 4. Reaching pylon 5, I would turn left back onto the course.

It was a lot of fun, and I was soon to achieve the moniker, Last Place Dan. When you are the slowest guy, you are popular with everyone. Don Beck won at 158.65 mph but was capable of much higher speeds.

The other racers were Tom Wrolstad in "Super Chic," Al Kramer in "Too Easy," and Dr. Robert Clark in "Love American Style." (A list of the competitors, their aircraft, and their speeds can be found in Appendix 1)

After the show on Sunday afternoon, I challenged Glen Earls in a Baby Great Lakes biplane to a dogfight. He had his ship on static display. We chased each other over the west side of the airport for about 15 minutes to the delight of the folks on the ground.

My call sign was "November 1 Papa Lima" or N1PL (Nipple). I picked a single number for a race number to paint on the tail—3. This was going to have a humorous consequence at my next race in Mojave, California.

June 20, 1976, California National Air Races, Mojave

The best I could do was 123.0 mph, but it was good enough for last place. Reno's Bar and Grill downtown would name specialty drinks after some of the competitors. They created a tequila with three strawberries and called it a Triple Nipple in my honor.

Big crowds. I watched Nick Jones and Ray Cote get into a fist fight over a rule in the Formula 1 class. Then Rare Bear, a heavily modified WWII Bearcat fighter in the Unlimited Division, landed gear up. The pilot, Lyle Shelton, had to manually crank down the gear during his emergency and didn't have enough altitude before touching down on that huge four-bladed propeller and his tailwheel.

The high point was the low level flyby of the United DC8 airliner flown by Clay Lacy with the Human Fly standing on top! I was hooked. I was flying with some of the best pilots in the country in an air show. I was going to need a faster ship. The prize money for last place was $171.11.

The Human Fly

Rare Bear

September 7–12, 1976, National Championship Air Races, Reno, Nevada

I was too slow to qualify for the field of 16 and was eliminated, but I did get to fly the course. A two-place "Starduster Two" flown by Norm Weis from Wyoming beat me out for the last spot. He later wrote a book about his experience entitled, *The Starduster* in which he mentioned beating "last place Dan" for the last slot in the field of 24.

Every one of my fellow competitors were colorful characters. Don Janson had been married and divorced five times. He told me his secret to success: "Every 4 or 5 years, find someone you don't like and buy 'em a house".

This was the last biplane race at Reno for several years. Politics had entered the race course. Don Beck was elected president of USARA and threatened the Reno Board of Trustees with a strike if the pilots did not receive a bigger purse. They reacted with a logical decision. The other three divisions, Unlimited, T6, and Formula Ones were invited back but not the biplanes. The other pilots saw the writing on the wall and capitulated to a non-sanctioned air race.

Holsclaw STOL Strip, Loomis, California

STOL means "Short Takeoff and Landing." The 1700-foot dirt strip was just five miles from the family ranch in Newcastle. It had 50-foot obstructions with trees on one end and power lines on the other at the King Road overpass on I-80. I climbed the big oak tree and put reflectors at the top in case I arrived at night. One night, I asked Dad to park on the end of the strip and shine his headlights down the dirt runway. I failed to tell him on which end to park. The standard approach was over the big oak tree, and he parked facing it from the other end. I had to land into the lights and couldn't see a thing.

I was allowed to use the little airport when I came home on weekends. In those days, liability had already become an issue, but Fritz and Claire Holsclaw were not concerned, and they allowed me to build a two-car garage at the far end of the strip to hangar my Smith-Miniplane. Wonderful people.

The Mong Sport Biplane

Joe Pribilo, a corporate pilot in Southern California, had an unfinished Mong biplane project for sale. Mongs have won more biplane races than any other design. Ralph Mong Jr., a simulator technician for American Airlines, had designed it based on the Rose Parakeet biplane of 1929. It was reduced to a wingspan of 16 feet and a length of 14 feet with a single seat and a Continental 65 hp engine.

There were no kits available for sale, just the blueprints. Every Mong was different having been modified by the builders. I bought the project and finished it with the help of Bud and Pearl Paulson who had built their own beautiful Starduster II. My ship had a shortened wingspan of 12 feet 6 inches. I installed a Lycoming IO-320,

160 hp engine with the help of Duke Dodge, a mechanic from Sacramento Sky Ranch.

There was no electrical system and no radio. It was strictly a VFR airplane. Fuel capacity was 18 gallons with two 4 gallon tanks in the upper wing; a 2 gallon header tank up forward, just aft of the firewall; and also an 8 gallon tank aft of the seat. With a burn rate of 8 gallons/hour, I had a two hour range with a 30 minute reserve at a comfortable 140 mph. Stall speed was 60 mph. Over the years, I accumulated 356 hours in the Mong, probably more than any other Mong pilot because I used it to commute to work.

September 8, 1977, First Flight

The first flight of the Mong took place on this date at the Holsclaw STOL Strip. I was off the ground in 200 feet and easily cleared the power lines. My landing only took 800 feet. The first flight was a success with no squawks.

January 9, 1978, Mexicali, Mexico

The next race was just across the border. I now had two biplanes, the Smith and the Mong. I invited Joe Williams to ferry the Smith and I raced both ships, in the gold and silver races. I took 5th place in the new Mong in the Championship race.

Top Row, left to right: Bill Cumberland, Tom Geygan, Al Kramer, Bill Nagle, Clem Fischer, Jerry Maracola, Don Fairbanks. Bottom Row, left to right: Bert Rathkamp, Don Beck, Dan Mortensen, Wayne Roe.

On Sunday afternoon, a Mexican Boeing 727 departed for Mexico City. We then lined up eight biplanes on the runway and took flight. Coming off the number 6 pylon for the straight-away in front of 20,000 spectators, we came nose-to-nose with a B727 opposite direction at 200 feet doing a flyby for the crowd.

Four of us went right and four of us went left of centerline. The 727 pilots did a nice wing-waggle and then pulled up for Mexico City. The crowd loved it. We were not too happy. A midair with a passenger jet would have permanently shut down air racing.

After landing, we called the control tower to complain. They denied any knowledge of the B727 coming back. Matter of fact, we were told that in the hot afternoons, they roll those big glass windows open for a little breeze and lie down on their serapes for a little siesta.

April 3, 1978, the Piper Pacer, N5926D

I traded the Smith for a four-place Piper Tri-Pacer project and converted it to a 150 hp taildragger known simply as Pacer N5926D with the help of Mike Benoist and Greg Toste. I test flew it on August 20, 1978. This ship became my standard commuter and family aircraft.

August 17 - September 6, 1978, California State Fair, Sacramento

Three of us were invited to exhibit our experimental aircraft. First, we had to demonstrate a short field takeoff and landing at the Lincoln Airport. We then landed in the 1,400 ft. west parking lot of the fairgrounds early Sunday morning with a Starduster biplane flown by Earl Browning, a Der Jager flown by Bob Connolly, and myself in my Mong biplane for the EAA Exhibit. A fire truck was standing by as a precaution. We flew the approach from the north and landed to the south.

December 3, 1978, Mexicali Again

It was a foggy overcast morning on the day of departure from the Holsclaw STOL Strip with an indefinite ceiling at about 300 feet. I figured I could find a hole in the cloud cover to climb to VFR on top of the stuff and then visually follow the California foothill airports southeast to Southern California.

Fritz Holsclaw and Greg Toste followed me on takeoff in his Waco SF260 for a few miles and then turned back when they saw me climb through a hole and disappear. Mike Benoist and his wife took off behind Fritz in my Pacer and immediately returned for a landing. I inadvertently found myself between cloud layers. Bad decision.

No choice but to continue southeast while looking for sunshine. Meanwhile, Fritz loaded everybody into his motor home and drove to Mexicali. We joined up the next day in Mexico.

I took what I thought was a southeasterly heading to parallel the central California valley but was actually flying south in a cold front. I overtook a Bonanza on an IFR flight plan. Rolled inverted and passed him bottom up. Must have been quite an experience for him. He was probably asking himself if he was upside down or the other airplane . . . and a little biplane flying faster than a speedy Bonanza would have been an insult to him.

No ground reference for over an hour between cloud layers, and I was concerned that if my heading was wrong, I could end up over the Pacific. Finally an occasional glimpse of Mother Earth but no recognizable landmarks. After 90 minutes, I broke into VFR weather (broken clouds) and sporadic sunshine, and I was still over California. What a relief.

Time to land and refuel but where? Spotted a paved crop duster strip and landed. It was Barrengo Mesa Farms; a private strip. There was nobody around. I found a five gallon can of auto gas in a shed, refueled, and left a note with a $5 dollar bill. I tied the tail to a fence, and hand-propped the engine.

My course now took me due east to Mojave. The pass through the Tehachapi Mountains from Bakersfield was socked in so I climbed to 15,300 to get over the cumulus clouds and then spiraled down over Mojave through breaks in the cloud cover. What a headache. Flying above 10,000 feet for more than a few minutes without sufficient oxygen is not conducive to your health.

I had a mobile home in Mojave because I was working at Edwards AFB at the time, so I parked the Mong in the hangar and went home to bed for the rest of the day, totally exhausted. I departed the next day for Mexicali with no further excitement.

Footnote: I am not a role model for young pilots. What I did was risky. Flying an open-cockpit biplane into weather with no instruments is foolish. It is an easy trap to fall into, particularly when other pilots put you on a pedestal based on your exploits. I'm alive in spite of myself and very lucky.

The race promoter put on a big dinner for us in town with live music. Fritz drove a full load of pilots and crew into town in the motor home. Dad and Howie Keefe, pilot of the P-51, Miss America, were in the back with a bottle of wine telling war stories. A good time was had by all.

I took second place behind Red Blackburn in a Pitts. I had the faster airplane and held back until the last lap to make the race look good for the crowd. Unfortunately, I gave Red too big a lead and couldn't catch him at the checkered flag. It was the only race Red ever won. He was ecstatic.

Tom Aberle Remembers

What fun we had at the Mexicali, Mexico air races in January and December. The trip down was a short one for me since I was based at the Compton airport in the Los Angeles basin. A friend in his 200 HP Pitts, and Don Perri from Tenino, WA, in #26 black Mong, traveled there together. Perri owned both his #26 Mong and the airplane I was flying, the old Boland Mong. We landed at Thermal for fuel and took off from the taxiway adjacent to the fuel pit which seemed reasonable to us.

Six years later, I spoke to a prior owner of the airplane I was flying, who asked "Did they ever find you?" Apparently Perri was a bit tardy in re-registering the airplane I was flying, and the Feds were on the hunt for our planes after our taxiway takeoff next to the FAA Flight Service Station at Thermal, California. The border crossing was a nonevent.

The Mexicali Airport Comandante was a jovial sort who embodied every facet of our FAA as well as airport manager. He informed us that we were to put on an air race and that he desired to make it possible and comfortable for us. We were to use the upwind half of the runway, while the approach end would be used by arriving/departing traffic. The exception was on Sunday when a Mexican B727 airliner would come and we'd be shut down for less than an hour.

On more than one occasion, I saw an aerobatic exhibition overhead, a flying clown act on the runway, and racing biplanes on the course, simultaneously. On Friday evening, our Comandante asked if we could fly some airplanes over downtown Mexicali to "stir up interest" and "please fly low and loud." Again, what innocent fun.

July 15, 1979, Cincinnati Regional Air Races, Lunken Airport, Ohio

One of my fellow biplaners, Don Fairbanks, owned a flight school, Cardinal Air Training, at Lunken Airport in Cincinnati, Ohio. He put together an air show with a biplane race and raised the purse money. Five of us from the West Coast flew together to Ohio.

Rendezvous at Carson City, Nevada

We were to meet in Carson City, on the morning of July 9. Fritz escorted me in the Mong with his Waco over the Sierra Mountains at dawn with dad along for the ride. Time en route was 48 very cold minutes in an open cockpit. We met Clem Fischer, Jerry Maracola, Don Beck, and Stan Brown. I couldn't get my engine started with Fritz pulling the prop for 30 minutes. I told the others to leave without me and I would catch up.

They were flying Interstate I-80, and it wandered around mountains to the north and east. I knew I could catch up by going straight line to the first refueling stop at Battle Mountain (BAM). I arrived there in 1 hour 6 minutes. They had just left. Refueled and departing BAM on a straight line course passing south of Elko through Secret Pass in the Ruby Mountains and south of Wells. That pass was absolutely beautiful with its alpine meadows and snow on the top. Time en route 1+30. I caught them at the next stop, Wendover, Utah. Wendover is an old WWII B29 training base on the edge of a dry lake bed.

Excitement Over Kankakee, IL

Beck was much faster in the Sorceress and would go on ahead to wait for us at each fuel stop. Of the four remaining no-radio ships,

I was the fastest ship and would bring up the rear in a loose formation matching the speed of the slowest aircraft, Jerry Maracola.

The next three days cross-country were uneventful until the evening of July 11. Jerry Maracola was afraid of getting lost and Clem Fischer had told him to just follow him. As we approached Kankakee at dusk, Stan Brown, who had the only map and was our leader, lost his map overboard. The  wind, through an open cockpit, ripped it right out of his hands. I noticed something flapping on his tail feathers but didn't know what it was.

Stan began to circle Kankakee in hopes of spotting the airport. Clem was low on fuel and took off to the southwest with Jerry on his tail, thinking that was where the airport was located. I stayed with Stan, not realizing he didn't know where he was going. In short order, we stumbled onto the Kankakee Airport below and landed in twilight. Don Beck was there waiting for us.

Our concern now was Clem and Jerry. They had found an old abandoned airport and landed. Don called the Highway Patrol to report two missing aircraft. Clem and Jerry hitched a ride, got a motel, and the next morning, emptied five gallons of auto gas into their tanks, and caught up with us at Kankakee.

After the Kankakee incident, I started carrying AAA road maps. Every little village in the country has a water tower with its name painted on the side. This is more detail than the aeronautical charts. Whenever I wanted to know where I was, I simply flew past the water tower and read the name and checked it against my AAA road map.

Shelbyville, Indiana

Our next stop for fuel was the Eagle Creek Airport in Indianapolis, then on to Cincinnati Lunken Airport. It began to rain after leaving Indy, and the four of us, with Clem in the lead, were forced down to about 200 feet to stay in ground contact. I was not comfortable with Clem pushing on in these weather conditions as we passed the Shelbyville Airport.

To my amazement, a radio tower went by extending up into the gloom. Now I'm concerned. Clem was our leader and said he had flown the route before. Everybody was to follow Clem, and obviously, the other three did not see the tower. What if there were more? I pushed up the power and on passing Clem, did a 180 degree turn in front of him back to Shelbyville. They all followed.

On landing, we pushed the four ships into a hangar and waited out the rain. The others verified they did not see the tower. On departure in VFR conditions later that day, we saw several more towers that would certainly have snagged one or more of us had we continued on. Total flying time en route from California to Lunken: 19 hours.

Clem Fischer

I took 4th place. WCPO-TV Channel 9 was a local sponsor. Beck's race number was 89 so he blocked out the "8" for this race. The WCPO helicopter was stationed in center field and filmed the race live from a hover and turning 360 degrees while focused on Beck in the lead so you don't see much of the rest of us on the video tape. The course was only 2 1/4 miles long so the FAA limited us to a maximum of 180 mph because of the proximity of the crowds to the race course.

Clem Fischer in his Mong, race number 8, rounded the number 6 pylon on the second lap and lost his propeller. It broke at the crankshaft flange putting him in a difficult situation. He landed on the runway directly under him at high speed and deliberately ground-looped the ship at the end to avoid hitting hangars.

Clem took a bus back to Carson City, to get another engine from a homebuilt that had flipped over on its back. He did not tear it down for inspection. He was short of cash and could not afford a total overhaul. This would have repercussions later.

Mike Benoist along with his wife, and my wife, Cheryl, airlined to Cincinnati and provided support as my pit crew. I met the FAA Flight Standards District Office manager who tried to talk me into transferring into his office from Air Traffic Control. I had applied for a transfer to Flight Standards when in August 1981 but the strike ended that.

Sep. 3, 1979 Cleveland National Air Races, Burke Lakefront Airport, Ohio

I left the Mong at Lunken and airlined home. Returned for the ship and flew to Cleveland in 2 hours for the next race which was the 50th Anniversary of pylon air racing.

Jimmy Doolittle

On Saturday afternoon after the heat race, I was under the Mong, cleaning up a hydraulic leak on the bottom of the fuselage while the crowds walked through the hangar looking at the race planes. When I got up, the crew next to me asked if I saw General Doolittle walk by with his entourage. I missed him. Doolittle had first flown in the National Air Races in Cleveland in 1929.

The Departure Out of Cleveland

Won fifth place on Sunday. Prize money was $430. Several of us wanted to start for home during a break in the airshow. Al Kramer, Bill Nagle, Dr. Wayne Roe, and I headed west, following Interstate 80 out of Ohio in light rain but good visibility. The plan was for Nagle and Roe to turn north once past Toledo and head for Kalamazoo. Kramer and I would continue west for California.

Roe had the only radio in his VOR-equipped Pitts and took the lead as navigator. He ran us right into the Toledo Airport control zone which requires radio contact. He had not called them. When I saw the airport, Kramer and I dove for the weeds hoping the tower would not see us. Never got a letter of inquiry from the FAA so if they did see us, they were not able to identify us.

We took the southern route because Kramer was based in Van Nuys. We separated in Bullhead City, Arizona. I next stopped in Mojave, California for fuel. If I wanted to win an air race, I would need a faster ship. Who better to talk to then Burt Rutan, the guru in the desert right there on the airport.

I walked in to the Rutan Aircraft Factory, met Mike and Sally Melville, who introduced me to Burt. He said he always wanted to design a racer and we shook hands on September 10, 1979. I provided the numbers on the fastest biplane at the time, the Sorceress, and Burt came up with three designs, two of which were radically-joined wing designs and unproven. I choose model 68 which resembled a Star Wars X-Wing Fighter which was more conventional and the rest is history. Burt designed the cockpit for his 6-foot-2-inch frame, but he never flew the aircraft. The design cost me $6000. I can't imagine what that would cost today.

Bad News

I had already arrived home in California when Stan Brown called to tell me Clem Fischer had died on takeoff at Sidney, Nebraska. Jerry Maracola and Clem had stopped there for fuel. Clem suffered engine failure and made two turns back to the airport, lining up with a taxiway. His glide was not sufficient to clear a hangar and he pulled the nose up, stalling the machine. There is still a hole in the concrete where he hit nose down. Clem was a pleasure to fly with. He was a veteran of 15 years of racing and a good man. He would give you the shirt off his back if you needed it.

There is a rule in the biplane class. Carry a brick. If the engine quits, throw it out. That's where you are going. The drag and high sink rate on a biplane with flying wires and struts is higher than most airplanes.

March 8, 1980, the Long-EZ Rollout

Burt added me to the guest list for the historic rollout of his new designs. On this day, he gave me the completed design study for the new racer and introduced the new Long-EZ prototype, N79RA, to the public. To my surprise, Burt invited me to ride along during the 30 minute demonstration and airshow for the news media and general public. I was privileged over the next several years to be invited to several more rollouts at Mojave including the Grizzly and Voyager.

June 15, 1980, 30th Annual Porterville Fly-in and Air Races, California

One of the problems we constantly had to deal with was counting the number of laps while racing on the course. It challenges your situational awareness of seven other airplanes in close proximity while keeping track of the laps we had completed. This was compounded by the fact that we didn't fly the same number of laps in each race. Some races were five laps and upward of ten on any given day depending on the time available between airshow aerobatics. All the contestants are full throttle from takeoff to the checkered flag. We would get a white flag at the home pylon starting the last lap.

Another challenging problem for us without radios was the recovery on the runway after the race. Should we land one at a time or can we do two aircraft on either side of the runway centerline? The controversy continues to this day. These little taildraggers are nose high in a three-point configuration on the ground and forward visibility is nil. You must use your peripheral vision to watch the edge of the runway as you roll out on landing while maintaining directional control.

The most exciting part of this air show was a grass fire which had everyone scrambling to move their airplanes. I finished in third place in the AMSOIL Special at 154.47 mph behind Pat Hines in the Sundancer and Al Kramer in the Cobra.

July 16, 1980, Junction City, Texas

I was en route to San Marcos, Texas for a race and landed late afternoon in Junction City to refuel. I had an hour to sunset and San Marcos was only an hour away. As I taxied to the run-up area, Tom Aberle showed up in the pattern. I had no idea he was in the area. On landing, something broke, and he lost control, flipping upside down.

I shut down and ran to him. He was yelling for someone to get him out and fuel was leaking. I couldn't lift the tail for him to escape. The fuel boy, the last guy on that little country airport, was just leaving for the day and saw the accident. He raced to the scene and helped me lift the tail high enough for Tom to drop out unhurt. We shared a motel room for the night. I flew the next morning to San Marcos. Several years later, I almost regretted saving him as he had a faster Mong and beat me in the championship at Reno.

Tom Aberle Remembers

"On my way to the San Marcos, Texas air races at the last refueling stop before my destination and who do I see? Danny Mortensen in his Mong in the run-up area. On landing rollout, I lose the left brake. The airplane goes off the runway and over on its back. I do what I can: mags, off; mixture, idle cut-off, fuel valve, off; can't remove the canopy so again, mags, off; mixture, idle cut, off; and so on 3 or 4 times until I hear someone near the tail of my airplane, so I yell, "HELP". Danny says "What do you want me to do?" I said "Lift the tail so I can get out." We get my broken airplane upright and into a lean-to hangar where it stays for about a week while I continue on to the races. I stayed well-lubricated for a couple days, then set about the task of getting my broken machine home. John Parker was there and had a spare tow vehicle headed west. We made

a deal and we got the airplane home. The rebuild brought about my successful "Long Gone Mong" which won the Gold at Reno in 1987 and 1989.

Tom continued to modify and improve the performance of his beautiful ship over the years, having now won a record 12 championships. In 2015, he broke his own record again with a speed of 284.454 mph in Phantom (formerly called Long Gone Mong).

July 20, 1980, Texas Championship Air Races, San Marcos

The Reno Board of Directors was considering bringing back the biplane races after a three year absence. They sent several board members to San Marcos to evaluate our race. We decided to put on a good show for them and agreed amongst ourselves to have everyone finish together on the last lap. Our prize money would be based on our qualifying times.

We only had nine airplanes. I was delayed due to weather as a result of helping Tom Aberle. I missed qualifying but was allowed to race by popular vote. Pat Hines in #1 Sundancer was damaged en route and did not show. Bob Hugo had the misfortune of a flat tire when he lined up for a heat race and did not qualify for the championship race. The Reno Board of Trustees was impressed with our race and we were invited back to the big party in 1980.

September 1, 1980, Cleveland Natl. Air Races, Burke Lakefront Airport, Ohio

On this trip east, I flew solo. On a "before sunrise" departure out of Cheyenne following Interstate 80 at 1,000 feet, I happened to see a fast-moving jet fighter pop up on a ridge line some three miles to my right and then disappear in the early morning shadows.

We were on an intercept course, and I'm watching now in case I have to descend or climb. The F4 phantom passed directly overhead clearing me by 100 feet before I could react. As I look to my left following the traffic, a second F4 passed directly below me by less than 100 feet. They were doing low level runs, and I doubt if they even saw me. My little Mong was not big enough to show on their radar scopes.

Sixth Place

I took sixth place and flew out on Monday morning for home. Uneventful flight with frequent stops every 1 1/2 to 2 hours for fuel. If there was no one to hand-prop me, I would tie the airplane to a fence and do it myself with the throttle cracked a quarter of an inch. There are no words to describe America from 1,000 feet. I am so thankful for the freedom to experience this. The only problem was a sore butt sitting in that seat all day from sunrise to sunset.

September 14, 1980, National Championship Air Races, Reno, Nevada

This would be my first race at the big show - Reno. I was too slow to qualify in 1976. I qualified number 11 in a field of 16 but had not prepared the Mong for racing. After prepping the ship the next day, I won the heat race at 157.48 mph, which was not fast enough for the gold race on Sunday.

I won the consolation race at 160.88 mph and was accused of sandbagging to drop down to the consolation race as opposed to finishing last in the gold. It was not intentional. I had arrived in Reno just in time to qualify and no time to install new sparkplugs or tape the drag areas on the ship.

It was during the championship race that Don Beck deliberately cut inside of two pilots on four different pylons in an attempt to break the world speed record for a closed course 3.1 mile track. Race rules require passes on the outside of the turn and/or above another contestant.

Don Fairbanks was angry at Beck having missed him by just a few feet. Fairbanks said he could see the rivets on the bottom of Beck's Sorceress as he went by. Fairbanks sat in his Knight Twister for 15 minutes after landing to cool off. Another pilot filed a protest, and Don was dropped to last place by the contest committee, giving the victory to Pat Hines.

By the way, a big "thank you" to Champion Spark Plugs and Shell Oil for their support at the air races. Champion would hand out free spark plugs, and Shell would provide a case of aviation oil every year.

May 31, 1981, Cincinnati Regional Air Races, Lunken Airport, Ohio

I was busy with the construction of the AMSOIL Rutan Racer and loaned the Mong to Keven Morris to race in Cincinnati. Keven took first place in Heat 1-A (the Silver Race) at 148.87 mph.

Aug. 4, 1981, the AMSOIL Rutan Racer, N301LS

The proposed design was put to a vote amongst the biplane racers before we started building. We got 23 yes votes, one "I don't know," and one no vote. Don Beck offered to sell the Sorceress to me for $30,000, but I wanted an original aircraft with my name attached to it from day one.

The Sorceress was designed and built by Lee Mahoney in 1970. When landing in Reno, Lee damaged a wingtip. The aircraft was grounded when it was determined to be unsafe due to a questionable repair. Don bought it, but it was always the Mahoney Sorceress. The Sorceress was a beautiful aluminum negative stagger-wing biplane and proved to be a very successful racing biplane with three national titles. It was the first racing biplane to exceed 200 mph. My new aircraft was designed based on specifications and performance numbers of the Sorceress.

Construction on the Rutan Model 68 began on
January 2, 1981 in the garage of Grady Houk connected
to a taxiway at the Sacramento Executive Airport.

On May 1, Burt hired my number one man, Larry Lombard,
to work full-time with him in Mojave. Duke Dodge was brought in
to manage the project as I was still with the FAA full-time. The other
employees included Mike Dilley, Kit Sodergren, and Mike Arnold—
all experts in composite construction.

Aircraft Construction

We were one of the first in general aviation to use vacuum-bag-
ging to cure the composites to reduce weight and increase strength. A
number of local volunteers from the Sacramento and Roseville EAA
(Experimental Aircraft Association) chapters pitched in to get experience in composite construction. The crew worked two shifts, seven
days a week, and finished the aircraft in seven months.

A foam core was used and we free-formed the cowl around the
Lycoming IO-320 A2B engine (160 HP). The wing planform was
designed for Burt by John Roncz. The wings were the key, designed
for speed in the turns. The Racer was designed to beat the fastest
airplane, the Sorceress, by 8 mph on the straight-away and 30 mph
in the turns.

Race rules required a strut between the two wings so a sexy,
curved I-strut was fashioned by Mike Arnold. It was installed only
for racing and removed for normal flight during the year.

Length and main wing were 22 feet. The canard (leading wing) was 18 feet 6 inches. A T-tail allowed the ship to turn at high G's while at the same time decreasing susceptibility to aero-elasticity. Gross weight was 1,126 pounds; empty weight, 854 pounds.

Because of the F-86 experimental fighter accident into the ice cream parlor at Sacramento Executive Airport a few years earlier, we were forced to truck the aircraft in one piece to Franklin Field some 10 miles south on an early Sunday morning with a police escort. Experimental aircraft were now forbidden to make test flights at Sac Exec. The first flight was on August 4 with no problems, and then I ferried the aircraft to the hangar at Lincoln, California to the north of Sacramento, accompanied by Larry Lombard in his VariEze as a chase plane.

AMSOIL Rutan Racer Specifications

Model 68 was a highly staggered, high aspect ratio configuration with the following advantages:

1) Decreased landing gear drag. The tires were in the canard wing tips.
2) The forward wing (canard) attached in a positive pressure gradient, reducing interference drag.
3) Higher span efficiency with lower induced drag due to vertical and horizontal separation of the wings.
4) Greater percentage of laminar flow in the prop wash.
5) Improved visibility over a conventional biplane because both wings were located below the pilot.

Construction: PVC foam core, carbon-glass fiber, and kevlar.
Propeller: Sensenich metal prop 66 x 66 inches.
Max engine RPM: 3750
Takeoff Distance 800 feet

Landing Distance 1,200 feet (no flaps)
Rate of climb 3,000 feet/minute
Ceiling 20,300 feet (demonstrated)
Cruise Speed 180 knots
Fuel Consumption 8 gallons/hour
Fuel Capacity 22 gallon main tank aft of cockpit
plus 15 gallons (7.5 on each side of the engine
cowl up forward) - Total 37 gallons.
Vr (rotate) 60 knots
Vne (never exceed) 300 knots (demonstrated)
Vs1 (stall speed) 55 knots (clean configuration)
Va (maneuver speed) 170 knots
Center of Gravity 6 - 25% of MAC (Mean
Aerodynamic Chord)
Cockpit Integrity 20 G's
Aspect Ratio 6.36
Wing area 76.5 square feet = 14.72 lbs/sq. ft.
Power loading 14.9

August 5, 1981, Test Flight, Day Two

The next day, on the first test flight of the morning and wearing
a parachute, I was exploring the stall envelope at 10,000 feet. This
marvelous ship would not stall. I would start a climb, hold full aft
stick, and the nose would drop straight ahead as the forward canard
wing would lose lift but the main (aft) wing did not. Upon reaching
level flight, the aircraft would again start to climb. I would continue
holding full aft stick, and the Racer would simply do this up and
down oscillation.

As per Burt, "Canard stall does not result in tumble or spin.
When the canard stalls, very strong restoring moments force the aircraft to maintain the natural limit angle of attack, a condition that
allows control instead of departure, and climb instead of mush. At
full aft-stick, there is a bobble as the aircraft seeks the designed angle.
Extensive flight tests conducted by NASA on the Long-EZ show that
any combination of sharp, repeated three-axis control inputs or even

tail slides do not produce divergence or departure from controlled flight. It is indeed a welcome feature to know that you can make a sharp turn to final, even slapping in full-aft stick, full rudder, and crossed aileron and not have the ground rise up to smite you."

I then tried a steep climbing turn into an accelerated stall, and the aircraft flipped over upside down into a tight spiral. This surprised me. I was totally unprepared for this. My first thought was that I had stalled the aircraft and Burt had said it was stallproof. I pulled the throttle to idle, took my right hand off the side stick and reached for the double latches on the left holding the canopy. I was going to leave the ship and join the caterpillar club using the parachute.

When I let loose of the side stick intending to bail out, the aircraft immediately stopped the spiral and began to recover to level flight with the nose coming up. I was only a second from disaster if I had opened the canopy. The aircraft lost 2,000 ft. in less than 3 seconds.

On the second test hop before lunch, the outside air temperature was now over 100 F and I was getting a lot of turbulence at 10,000 feet. I decided to climb to cooler air and began a slow climb. 30 minutes later, I was at 20,300 feet and started back down for lunch.

Sitting in the shade of the hangar looking at the nose of the ship, it appeared to be unevenly parked on the ramp. Closer inspection found a large crack in the left canard (forward wing) close to where it joined the fuselage.

We anticipated some heat from the short exhaust stacks across the canard less than two feet behind and had fashioned asbestos material under a stainless steel plate on the left wing. Unfortunately the heat flow pattern in an extended climb changed to a wider area across the wing beyond the protective plate, and *melted* the composite spar. The slow descent in the cold air at altitude allowed the composite material to solidify by the time I landed.

A call to Burt brought him up from Mojave to inspect the damage the next day and instruct us on how to repair the ship. We cut away the damaged portion, repaired the spar and foam core, adding 30 percent more material to the wing.

We had to also add 30 percent to the canard on the other side of the fuselage for balance. We missed Oshkosh but made Reno with only 18 hours on the airframe. The FAA required 25 hours of flight test before leaving the area but who's counting?

Burt

September 17, 1981, National Championship Air Races, Reno, NV

I arrived in Reno with the new AMSOIL Rutan Racer and on the first practice hot lap, I was clocked unofficially at 236 mph by

Jack Sweeney, 13 mph faster than the world record. There was no other traffic on the course to impede my speed.

Controversy arose when Al Kramer and Pat Hines arrived with smaller tires than allowed in the 1976 rules. They insisted a vote had been taken, allowing the change, but nobody recalled any such vote nor could they produce a newer set of rules. In the end, however, they were allowed to race.

I qualified officially in second place at 211.25 mph with other traffic on the course. I also qualified the Mong, new race number 03, which I subsequently raced in the Silver Race (the second group of eight ships).

The NASA Laminar Flow Study

Burt and Dick Rutan, Jeana Yeager, and Mike and Sally Melville from Mojave had flown in for the race. Burt and Dr. Bruce Holmes of NASA (National Aeronautics & Space Administration) were involved in a laminar flow study and on Tuesday evening, September 14th, asked me to do a test flight after the airshow. They sprayed a sublimating chemical on the airfoils and instructed me to fly about 15 minutes at 70 percent power.

The applied solution slowly changed to a frost-like appearance with narrow V-shaped patterns developing back across the wing wherever there was a loss of lift due to pinholes in the paint finish and bug strikes on the leading edges.

The study involved eight aircraft including a Learjet, VariEze, Long-EZ, Bellanca Skyrocket-II, Cessna P210, Beech 24R Sierra, Beech T34C, and my aircraft. We were surprised that there was no loss of lift over the canard (leading wing) within two feet of the propeller diameter and subsequent prop wash. My airfoils had laminar flow to 61 percent of the wing chord.

Al Kramer complained that the spraying of the sublimating chemical on my wings in the biplane hangar had contaminated his aircraft. NASA explained to him that there was no overspray on his aircraft, and Kramer couldn't prove it. Some people are so short-sighted that they cannot see the big picture. It was a research study for the advancement of aviation and he was embarrassingly self-centered.

The Heat Race

On Thursday, the first day of heat racing, I cut the number three pylon on the third lap. My affected time was 210.92 mph with the penalty behind Pat Hines in Sundancer at 224.90. It dropped me to sixth place. Nevertheless, it qualified me for the gold race on Sunday.

September 20, 1981, the Championship Race

Just before the Championship Race on Sunday, I was informed by Kramer and Hines that they would file a protest if I raced with AMSOIL synthetic oil. Synthetics had been used by Don Beck in the Mojave race and allowed by voice vote. Why did they wait until Sunday morning knowing all week that I was using a synthetic oil and had a sponsor who funded the ship? I had discovered that being competitive no longer made me the most popular pilot.

I told them that AMSOIL was interested in sponsoring some races with prize money and this would kill the deal. This made no difference to them. They felt threatened by a fast airplane. They perceived an advantage which I freely admitted and offered to sell them some product.

I checked with Wally Beug, the AMSOIL VP who was present, and at the risk of being disqualified after the race, we decided to change oil back to the Aeroshell petroleum oil. I've always regretted doing this in hindsight. The new synthetic (composite) racer with the big AMSOIL logo on the side got us just as much publicity nationwide in spite of them.

On one lap, coming off of pylon 3, I almost collided with Doug Kempf and Dennis Brown in two identical Pitts. I had looked at them as I took pylon 1. They were passing pylon 3 ahead of me in formation. I then looked at pylon 2 to get as close to it as possible and was surprised coming off pylon 3 by my closure speed on Doug and Dennis.

My ground track took me right between the two of them with just feet to spare in a 70 degree bank. If they had been flying their formation any tighter, I would have hit both of them. This was the first time I had lapped anyone at a high rate of speed. They were doing 143 mph, and I was running nearly 100 mph faster. I was shocked and totally unprepared by my closure rate with slower traffic.

I experienced wake turbulence coming off pylon six on the fourth lap and was spilled inside the course. I was able to recover just above the sagebrush, but rather than turn hard right, back to the course before reaching the home pylon where the timers and judges were located, I elected to fly directly to the number 1 pylon. I was concerned that a hard right turn into following traffic prior to the home pylon at stage center would be too dangerous.

I was not aware that cutting inside the home pylon was a penalty and I actually flew a greater distance than if I had stayed on the course. I crossed the finish line at 206 mph, just 3 mph slower than Pat Hines. The penalty was 48 seconds which dropped me to third place.

Back on the ramp, Burt met me as I was shutting down the engine and asked what happened on pylon six. I told him wake turbulence and he told me to stay put. He then held the aileron on the main wing and asked me to move the side stick (I didn't have a center-mounted stick on the floor). He was easily able to hold the aileron while I exercised full movement. The 5/8th aluminum tubing connecting the controls were flexing inside the wing at high speed and I was only getting 6 degrees of travel versus the designed 12 degrees.

I ferried the Racer to Mojave for Dick Rutan and Mike Melville to evaluate and Dick commented he didn't see how I could maintain control on the race course at all. I didn't think it was difficult. We replaced the tubing with steel rod to solve the problem and increased the aileron movement to 24 degrees by creating more room for the right-hand side stick to move to the right instead of bumping into the interior side of the cockpit.

October 19, 1981, San Marcos, Texas

Due to weather, only three biplanes showed and two of them were mine. The AMSOIL Rutan Racer; my Mong flown by Bob Metz; and Alan Preston with his Pitts biplane. The Formula 1 aircraft had a full field because they trailered their aircraft to the races.

I was the fastest qualifier in the AMSOIL Rutan Racer and took first place. Missed breaking the world speed record for a three mile course by one or two seconds when I had to go wide on the last pylon to get around the slower ships I had lapped.

Bob Metz had another airplane to pick up in Texas so we left the Mong in the hangar with the intent for me to airline back to get it later. A few months later, I was informed by Sacramento FAA inspector Jerry Redman that he had seen my Mong doing low-level aerobatics at the Woodland Airport ten miles west of Sac Metro. I told him the Mong was in Texas and he insisted it was back. Metz had returned to Texas on business and without my knowledge or permission, had picked up the Mong and flown home. I was upset because I had allowed the insurance to lapse.

FAA Abuses

The FAA wanted to take enforcement action on Metz for several reported infractions including dropping parachutists from his Twin Beech BE18 from on top of an overcast into Woodland, and allegedly running drugs from Mexico. They asked me to file a stolen aircraft report and then they would charge him with that since they couldn't prove the other allegations. I refused but not out of any loyalty to Metz. I was happy to just get the Mong back in my hangar.

Over the years, I have seen the FAA from the inside take a personal vendetta against a few pilots. Case in point, Bill Paynter of Union Flights at Sac Executive was harassed by the FAA for years at a cost of thousands of dollars to defend himself. Bill was a staunch proponent of aviation and an icon in the community. Whether he was guilty of an infraction, I have no idea but it certainly appeared to be a personal attack on the part of the FAA from where I stood.

Another situation years later involved Bob Hoover, a WWII vet and test pilot, and perhaps one of the most famous personalities in aviation. Two FAA inspectors observed his airshow routine in his Shrike Commander and wrote him up for unsafe flying. The press went bananas. The two inspectors were accused of trying to make a name for themselves by grounding Mr. Aviation. He got his certificates back but, again, at a cost of many thousands of dollars and eventually went back on the airshow circuit.

October 21, 1981, Duluth, MN to Lincoln, California

Departed Duluth for Lincoln in the Racer at sunrise with two fuel stops, Ogallala, Nebraska and Salt Lake Number 2, Utah. Distance 1,850 miles and 12.5 hours flight time. Fuel stops took 45 minutes for snacks and the restroom. Made it by sunset. Average speed 141 mph at 2400 rpm.

November 19, 1981, ABC Good Morning America

Channel 13 TV, Sacramento, asked if they could film the AMSOIL Rutan for a local segment. We did some flying with their helicopter film crew at Lincoln. The video was picked up the next day on the national morning show and got AMSOIL about six minutes of national coverage.

December 8-22, 1981, Chuck Andrews

Chuck was a retired Air Force Major who flew B47s and then a C47 gunship in 'Nam. He was recommended for the Medal of Honor for evacuating wounded one night under fire in his overloaded C47 on a short unlit landing strip in the jungle. He was president of USARA prior to my election. Chuck had three world speed records in "Real Sporty," a Cassutt in the Formula One Division and was the recipient of the FAI "Louis Bleriot" award in Paris.

The Federation Aeronautique Internationale in Switzerland was created in 1905 by the Olympic Congress as the sanctioning body for aviation. In 1922, the National Aeronautics Assn. (NAA) in Washington, DC was created as the US representative for certification of air records.

Chuck invited me to fly right seat with him in the company King-Air out of Beckley, West Virginia. I spent a month with him and also received five hours of dual in the Hughes 500D helicopter. I got to a point where I could almost hover.

Thanks to Chuck, I was awarded with a King-Air one-week ground school at the Beech factory in Wichita a few months later. At the graduation ceremony, I had the pleasure of lunch with Olive Ann Beech and Linden Blue. They were very interested in Burt Rutan and quizzed me extensively about him and composites. They later entered into a contract with him to introduce composites in their production line; the result being a new turboprop twin, the Starship.

March 11, 1982, Moderate Turbulence

Out of El Paso, Texas headed east, I encountered moderate turbulence at 6,000 feet and my head was bouncing off the canopy (I was wearing my Army crash helmet). This, along with the sun beating down on me made for a very uncomfortable ride. I landed on a crop duster strip in west Texas and laid down in the shade to recover from the urge to barf.

Feeling better, I called Burt and asked him about a turbulence penetration speed. There was nothing in the design specifications about this. He asked how fast I was going. I said, "About 170 mph" and he said, "That's it." Obviously the ship held together and I had just demonstrated a valid number.

March 12, 1982, Aileron Reversal

On this date, I delivered the AMSOIL Rutan Racer to Chuck Andrews in Beckley, WV. Cheryl and I were expecting our first child and Chuck took the Racer to the Sun 'n' Fun airshow in Lakeland, Florida. The aircraft won Best New Design. Chuck was my backup pilot and his name is prominently displayed under my name on the side of the cockpit in the EAA Museum in Oshkosh, Wisconsin.

On the way there, Chuck did some flight tests. He put the aircraft into a dive and at approximately 300 mph, experienced aileron reversal. The B47 had the same problem so he knew exactly what to do. He used opposite control input to recover. I chided him for not wearing a parachute when he told me about the test flight.

April 27, 1982, Multi-Engine ATP Checkride

Passed my multi-engine Airline Transport Pilot checkride with Bob Crass, Manager of the Sacramento FAA in a Piper Seminole.

May 1, 1982, the First World Speed Record Attempt

Chuck Andrews invited me to attempt the 3 kilometer world speed record for my weight class, C.1.b. for propeller-driven aircraft on the official NAA course that was established at Beckley, West Virginia. The local EAA chapter volunteers manned the timing booths at each end of the course. Don Berliner represented the NAA as official judge.

The record was held by Capt. Barry Schiff (TWA) and Hal Fishman of KTLA-TV, Channel 5, Los Angeles in a Siai Marchetti SF260 (aka Waco Meteor) with 260 horses. The AMSOIL Rutan Racer only had 160 horsepower.

I was highly optimistic but you know what they say... "Optimism is going after Moby Dick with a rowboat and taking the tartar sauce with you." The first attempt was not successful. I had to exceed the record by one per cent. That afternoon we stripped the ship of all excess weight, drained excess fuel, reset the timing on the magnetos, and applied lots of drag reduction tape.

On May 2, my fastest lap was 241 mph and I broke the record with an average of 234.64 mph. I did 10 passes through the timing gates and completely forgot about fuel. One more pass and I would have run out of fuel. This record would not have been possible without Chuck Andrews, my mentor, who suggested the speed record attempt; Don Berliner, the official NAA observer; and the local EAA volunteers. Thanks, guys.

Left to right: Danny, Chuck, & Don Berliner.

We lost Chuck a few years later while test-flying a new aircraft design for Jimmy Miller in Texas. On a high speed run, the wooden prop broke and cut off the t-tail on a pusher design airplane. Chuck was not wearing a chute.

July 18, 1982, Piper Super Cub on Floats

John Ortman, a Northwest Airlines captain, operated the Fixed Based Operation in Duluth Harbor (Sky Harbor Airport) and taught in a 150 hp Super Cub on floats. I received 7.5 hours of dual from him and then took a commercial single-engine sea checkride. If you have never flown on the water, you don't know what you are missing. It is simply exhilarating much like an open cockpit.

August 13, 1982, Lightning Strike

I was inbound to Superior, Wisconsin with low ceilings and rain. In the vicinity of Eau Claire, I experienced a lightning strike directly in front of me and immediately diverted into Eau Claire which had a Flight Service Station. No damage to the composite structure. It began to rain hard as I landed with a thunderstorm overhead. I didn't see that coming. The FSS specialist questioned my arrival in IFR conditions without a radio call. I told him the lightning strike toasted the radio or I would have declared an emergency. I got totally soaked running 50 feet into the terminal in the downburst.

September 16-18, 1982, National Championship Air Races, Reno, Nevada

On my first practice run on Monday, September 13th, I swallowed an exhaust valve. Sacramento Sky Ranch brought up another cylinder for me and on Tuesday, another exhaust valve failed. We had failed to find all the broken pieces in the engine from the first incident. Sky Ranch to the rescue again with four new cylinders the next day. I finally qualified in second place on Wednesday at 212.3 mph. The trials and tribulations of racing.

The Dogfight

On a test flight after the show on Saturday evening, I initiated a dogfight with a Marine OV10 that was loitering over the field. We chased each other around for about 10 minutes to the enjoyment of everyone on the ground. About four months later, I got a letter from the Marine Corps inquiring about an OV10 involved in unauthorized aerobatics. I ignored it. Hope those guys didn't get a reprimand.

The Racing Biplane Class

This was the year that we broke the Sport Biplane Class into two groups. Several aircraft were lapping the slower contestants and the closure rate on the course had become unsafe. A new class, the Racing Biplane class was created with the following pilots and aircraft:

Pat Hines in Sundancer, Race #1
Don Beck in Sorceress, Race #89
Danny Mortensen in the AMSOIL Rutan Racer, Race #3
Al Kramer in Cobra, Race #22
Tom Aberle in Two Bits, Race #25

Pat Hines Jumps the Start

In the championship race, Pat Hines jumped the start and should have been penalized but the starter did not report the infraction to the race committee back at race headquarters. At full power waiting for the green flag to drop, we had pit crew members hanging on to the wingtips and tail. The brakes would not hold us. Pat's crew lost their hold on the airplane and he jumped out ahead of the start line by several hundred feet before he could stop.

We all passed him on the start and I cautiously took the lead from Don Beck on the fourth of six laps. I took too much time to pass Beck in the Sorceress; the ship that we were designed to beat. I didn't know that Hines was gaining on me. On the last pylon, number six, for the checkered flag, I looked behind me for Pat and inadvertently went wide in the turn. Pat was high and managed to dive ahead of me between the pylon and me. He beat me in a photo finish by less than a second.

Not too worry. He jumped the start which is a penalty. I never thought to walk up to race headquarters to check the posting. The announcers, having seen the violation, announced me as the winner, assuming a penalty would be assessed. Contestants have one hour after a race to file a protest which cost $100. Hours later I learned that the infraction had not been reported and Pat was awarded first place. Pat got the coveted Breitling watch too. It was a hard lesson.

Pat officially finished the six laps on Sunday in 5 minutes, 20.80 seconds at 209.401 mph. I completed the course in 5 minutes, 21.10 seconds = 209.206 mph. Pat had the faster airplane, but the infraction on the start line should have penalized him a lap. Victory goes to the pilot who makes the next-to-the-last mistake.

Kudos to the pit crew who campaigned with me: Larry Lombard, Mike Dilley, Mike Arnold, Kit Sodergren, Duke Dodge, Ed Popejoy, Larry Beck, Larry Lathrop, and Lennie Evans. Without them over the years, I would never have been successful on the pylons.

October 1, 1982, A World Altitude Record

AMSOIL sent me to the Dulles 400 mile efficiency race in Virginia, but the weather was bad with rain on Saturday morning, so the race was postponed to Sunday. While sitting around the FBO and talking with Steve Oster, owner and pilot of a Ted Smith twin-engine Aerostar 601P, I suggested we do a world record attempt in his aircraft with the AMSOIL synthetic 20W50 automobile racing lubricant.

We had the new AVOIL on the market but not available this day. I was still using the 20W50 automotive synthetic racing oil in my ship with excellent results and that was readily available.

Col. Milt Brown, Secretary of the NAA was present with the record book and we discovered that no record attempt had ever been made for the absolute altitude in horizontal flight in weight class C.1 Group 1 for piston-engine aircraft. He had a barograph with him and it was installed in the ship to verify the required 15 kilometer level run at altitude.

Weldon Britton, the local FAA chief, was present and arranged for Washington ARTCC (Center) to track us when we called for the attempt at altitude. They would record the radar return on video tape.

We went on oxygen as we climbed and we turned off the pressurization in the cockpit to get more horsepower to the engines.

It took us 1 hour 30 minutes to get to 33,000 feet and we were hanging on the props. The aircraft started to buffet and Steve pushed the nose down to avoid a stall. We recovered and climbed back to 31,800, called the Center and started our run. The air traffic controller assigned to us just for this record attempt, verified 15 km in level flight and we got a clearance to descend. It only took 30 minutes to get back down but now Dulles was below landing minimums in heavy rain.

Steve had his Aerostar certified for Category II ILS approaches. A standard ILS Category I approach is a 200 foot ceiling and a minimum 1/2 statute mile visibility. Cat II is 100 and 1/4. We did a Cat II approach to Dulles.

The pressurized Aerostar is only certified to FL250 (25,000 feet). When we got back to the FBO, Weldon informed us he was going to have to violate us for flying above the manufacturer's service ceiling. He was joking but had not thought of this before we departed. He wrote the waiver letter authorizing us to exceed the limitations on the airplane on Monday when he got back to his office. A few weeks later, we were notified that the FAI had certified the record.

*The NAA is the US representative of the FAI in Paris and is the equivalent of the Olympics for aviation. To attempt a record requires a fee and a window of 90 days in which to make the attempt(s). NAA officials must be present at the time of the attempt. If you are interested in a US or world record in your logbook, contact the NAA at www.naa.org.

October 10, 1982, Second World Speed Record

I learned there was an NAA-sanctioned 75 km course from Leesburg, Virginia to Warrenton, Virginia and back. With the help of the local EAA chapter volunteers to man the timing checkpoints, I attempted the 100 km closed course record for C.1.b piston-engine aircraft in the AMSOIL Rutan Racer. This class is based on weight between 1,000 and 2,000 pounds. I operating at the minimum weight and ran the course at 500 feet AGL to get as close to the checkpoint in the turn at the far end of the course.

In making the 180 degree turn (70-degree bank) at Warrenton at approximately 250 mph, I pulled so many Gs that I almost passed out with blood draining to my lower extremities. I could see the wings bending. Thank goodness for strong graphite wings. Lost a lot of speed in the turn which dropped me to an average of 233.32 mph for a second world speed record for AMSOIL.

Jan. 15, 1983, Flying on Skis

It snows hard and deep in Wisconsin in the winter and it gets very cold. Not much opportunity to fly. Bob Ortman checked me out in the Super Cub on skis at Sky Harbor in Duluth. I did not enjoy flying without a heater and froze my you-know-what in the process. What was I thinking?

March 16, 1983, The Blizzard

On a flight from Superior, Wisconsin to Reno, Nevada, I encountered a fast-moving cold front and snow showers following Interstate 15 south from Butte, Montana. Crossed the Continental Divide at 500 feet AGL (Monida Pass is 6823 feet) with weather deteriorating. If it got any worse, I planned to turn around only to discover it was now worse behind me (and very cold). I didn't have a heater in the racer.

A small town appeared below and I landed in an open patch of snow-covered ground as the ceiling and visibility dropped to zero. Rough landing but no damage to the aircraft. Walked about one-half mile to the nearest building. Turned out to be a cafe and discovered that I had landed on an airport. Everything covered in several inches of snow and there was nothing to indicate I was on a little country airport.

Spent an hour thawing out and the weather improved to VFR with occasional bursts of sunshine. The locals gave me directions to the snow-covered runway. I swept the snow off the wings and departed Dubois, Idaho for Idaho Falls. Venturing into weather is like sticking your head in the mouth of a lion to see if he is hungry. Dodged another bullet. Time en route to Reno was 11 hours; half the time it took in the old Mong.

I was asked recently if I filed VFR flight plans with the Flight Service Station on my cross-country flights. I confess the answer is no. I don't like making plans for the day because then the word *premeditated* gets thrown around the courtroom.

June 6, 1983, Propeller Failure

Volk Field is a National Guard base at Camp Douglas, Wisconsin. with runways 9/27. Preparing to depart Beckley, West Virginia after an airshow, I discovered that I had a dead battery. A big ol' farm boy in bib overhauls volunteered to hand-prop my aircraft while I sat in the cockpit to work the throttle.

About two hours later, as I passed over Volk Field at 6000 feet at 4 p.m. en route to Superior, Wisconsin, 18 inches of prop blade broke off. I was running hard (2850 RPM and 200 mph) to beat a line of thunderstorms approaching the Duluth-Superior area from the west.

Oil and fuel lines broke. The ship shuddered violently for about four seconds as I reached for the throttle. The engine broke loose from the engine mount. All the instruments on the panel broke and I lost electrics—no radio, and no parachute! I had finished the test program; a chute was no longer required.

The engine was still in the cowl but hanging at a downward angle, secured to the airframe by the required 3/16-inch wire cable as per the race rules. The cable ran back through the Kevlar fire wall. If it were not for that cable, the engine would have separated from the ship and I would have lost control due to an out of "center of gravity" scenario.

That 9,000-foot runway below me was the most beautiful thing I had ever seen. I pushed the nose down to descend and as my speed increased, the engine began flopping around inside the nonstructural two-ply fiberglass cowl. Back to level fight and no choice but to let the speed bleed off and then descend more slowly. It took 10 minutes to get down to the runway in a shallow glide.

It was Monday afternoon and the National Guard didn't have anyone in the traffic pattern. I passed silently over some workers on the end of the runway at 100 ft AGL and they didn't even notice me. I rolled to an intersecting taxiway and turned off the runway.

Climbed out, looked at the damage, and then hiked into Base Ops and declared an emergency. I asked if I could push the airplane into a hangar and would I be required to trailer the aircraft out. They directed me to a hangar with F16s and said I could repair the AMSOIL Rutan Racer there and fly it out.

I called Al Amatuzio, president of AMSOIL and gave him the good news and the bad news. I was alive but the ship was badly damaged. The narrow part of the fuselage where it connects to the tail had a vertical crack of 180 degrees across the top and sides. Another second or two of vibration and the tail would have snapped off!

I caught the Greyhound bus from Eau Claire to Superior. Called Sacramento Sky Ranch to order a new engine and flew in Duke Dodge from California six weeks later to install the engine and repair the fiberglass damage.

In analyzing the prop, we discovered a large scratch across the front of the blade which had occurred when the volunteer farm boy had hand-propped me. He was wearing a large ring on his hand which scratched the prop.

Another factor was a slight vibration whenever I passed through 2900 RPM with this particular prop. Obviously a harmonics problem, so I avoided operating at that speed. Even though I did not feel a prop vibration at 2850 rpm, the prop was weakened by the scratched surface.

September 13, 1983, A New Race Propeller

I picked up a new Sensenich metal prop from Ted Burrows at Aero Propeller in Long Beach, California built to my specs, a 66 x 66 for a cash sale out the back door. He was concerned about liability. Propellers are a black art. He would take a blank prop, heat-treat it, thin the blade, and bend it to my specs. The new prop did not turn up like the one I destroyed which had consequences at the next race.

Why a 66-inch diameter by 66-degree pitch? Those were the prop numbers that Don Beck was flying when he broke the race course record in 1982. I peeked at his prop when he had the spinner off during maintenance. I didn't know what RPMs he was pulling but I was getting 3750 RPMs out of that Lycoming engine which was rated at 2750 RPMs. We did that by adjusting the magneto timing,

September 15–18, 1983, National Championship Air Races, Reno, Nevada

This was going to be my year. We had great expectations even though I had lost my racing prop a few weeks earlier. I arrived on Monday, Sep. 12, the first day of qualifications. I qualified on Wednesday in third place at 210 mph.

The Windecker Kevlar Propeller

Jerry Redman of the Sacramento FAA, and a former air traffic controller, mentioned that Ted Windecker had an experimental adjustable composite 13 pound Kevlar blade that I should try. Jerry had worked for the Windeckers when they were building the Windecker Eagle some 10 years earlier. I bought the prop for $1500. We had it shipped overnight.

It was installed along with a composite spinner they provided. I attempted a practice lap to test the performance but on takeoff, the spinner disintegrated. It turned out that it was not an airworthy spinner. It had been built for static display. I aborted the takeoff.

I arrive on the ramp after the aborted
takeoff with the loss of the spinner.

Jerry asked if he could borrow the prop to do some research on possibly manufacturing a similar prop. Shortly thereafter, he was killed in a gyrocopter accident, and I was not able to locate with whom he was working on the project. A great opportunity and a prop lost to history!

September 17, 1983, Last Minute Changes

It was Saturday morning, and we had a heat race scheduled at 11 a.m. The Sensenich metal prop was not turning the RPMs I needed. I had been experimenting with several other props before and after the airshow each day.

The pit crew was up late that night working on the engine hoping to fine-tune it for more RPMs and I felt obligated to stay up with them. I should have gone to the motel and slept. I was tired and fatigued the next morning with little sleep and my reaction time was slow.

One of the little tricks to get another 50–100 rpm in the championship race was to take a hacksaw to the prop tips and remove 1/4 inch and then file to a smooth finish. It worked, and since we were only on the course for 10 minutes, the risk was minimal. Only did it three times in my career. The prop would be removed and sent to the prop shop after the race to be balanced. If you never try anything new, you will miss out on many of life's great disappointments.

The Morning Pilot Briefing

Following the mandatory briefing at 8 a.m. on Saturday morning, I told my fellow racers that I was not going to fly the heat race - too tired. I had a slot in the championship race on Sunday. They insisted I fly and Pat Hines offered me another prop to test in the heat race. The opportunity was too great to pass up.

Then while watching the KC135 Air Force tanker and four F4 fighters do a "flyby" to start the show at 9 a.m., Pat Hines, standing next to me, said, "Look at that big tanker. It looks like it is hardly moving because it is so large. We have the same situation on the race course. You are larger than the rest of us, and we have a problem judging our closure speed on you." This would have serious consequences two hours later.

The Heat Race

Wind gusts were 30 knots from the southwest. The race officials asked if we wanted to cancel the race. We felt we were good enough (pilot ego) to deal with the wind. It necessitated a takeoff to the west on Runway 8 opposite our normal takeoff. We were to fly to a scatter pylon on the west side of the airport and then do a 180 degree left turn back to the straight-away in front of the bleachers and timing booth and then fly a left pattern around the course.

Normal takeoffs are on Rwy 26 and then directly onto the course in a left traffic pattern around the pylons. North is at the top of the following diagram. The smallest circle is the 3.1 mile track for the Biplanes and Formula Ones. The black dots represent the 35 foot pylons with red and white 55 gallon drums mounted on top.

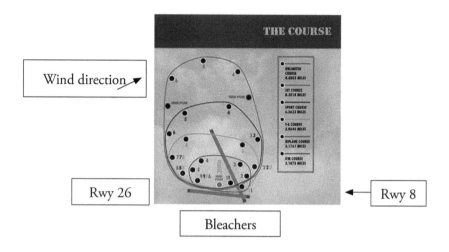

The prop I had borrowed from Pat Hines got me off the ground first on the race horse start, but the aircraft did not accelerate well. I stayed low, about 35 feet, to build speed. Upon reaching the scatter pylon, everybody had caught up with me. I was in a test flight mode and not concerned about the race.

Don Beck passed just below and outside of me at the scatter pylon and as he legally passed, he started a climbing left turn to get above the pylon height of 35 feet. I saw his right wingtip out of the corner of my eye and lost a precious second as I contemplated what he was doing. I was forced into the turn to avoid him and wondered if I had passed the scatter pylon on my left, having looked in the direction of Don on my right.

As I rolled into the left turn, I now had a direct headwind of 30 knots and was accelerating through 200 mph. I passed directly behind Don following in trail and experienced his wake turbulence causing me to roll uncontrollably past 90 degrees of bank. I attempted to recover with aileron and elevator. I was able to pitch the nose up but the ailerons were useless. I was unable to arrest the sink rate from his downwash.

On the race course, we frequently experience wake turbulence from the other aircraft but easily recover with only a slight wing rock and roll as we pass through the rough air. Today I was following in the same ground track of Beck with a direct headwind. As I sank toward the ground, I thought, "Lord, I wanna play let's make a deal" followed by the realization that this was going to be instantaneous at this speed and wouldn't hurt.

Don and me

The ship is traveling right to left.

I impacted in a knife-edge attitude with the left wings absorbing the crash. I hopped, skipped, cart-wheeled, and tumbled through the desert for 1,000 feet before coming to a stop. Total time from impact to stop was 7 seconds. Burt had designed the cockpit for 22 G's in case something went wrong. I had removed the instruments, G-meter, radio, etc. to reduce weight for the race and I don't know how many G's I actually incurred.

Race Number 3 is Down

The air show announcer, Danny Clisham, made that call to the spectators. For those who had been in Reno in 1979 when Steve Hinton had crashed in the P51 Red Baron and had heard a similar announcement, it brought a flood of emotion and gasps from the crowd. The airport came to a standstill and with only the sounds of the crash trucks rolling. The worse was assumed.

A big cloud of dust. I couldn't see anything and I think I closed my eyes on impact. I thought of my family as I realized I was going in. I didn't know if I had a control linkage failure to the ailerons or wake turbulence. From the time I lost control to impact was less than three seconds.

The dust cleared and I realized the aircraft had stopped. My next thought was surprise that I was alive and now I might burn to death in the cockpit.

The ship was lying on its side as the dust settled and I was looking at the ants in the sand. I hit the quick five-point Indy seat belt release and pushed out through the broken canopy. The engine had separated during the last second and broke the enclosed canopy, missing me by an inch as it bounced over me.

Paul Poberezny, EAA president remarked that "Nobody could live through what I just saw" and race veteran Steve Wittman, upon hearing that I was alive, said, "Well, now I've seen several miracles."

I started to run from the aircraft and tripped over the mixture control cable attached to the engine. That's when I got hurt. The engine had separated from the airframe and was laying some five feet away. It was still connected to the ship by the cable. I didn't see it. Stood up and realized it wasn't going to burn. I took off my crash helmet and my Nomex suit and put them in the airplane.

I could hear the freeloaders on the west airport fence line cheering when they saw me exit the airplane. The Crash, Fire, Rescue trucks arrived about five minutes later. The first EMT out of the truck thought I was one of the spectators from the fence. I was wearing a white shirt and black slacks and certainly did not look like a race pilot.

Denial

I didn't want to have anything to do with the accident. The paramedic asked if I had seen the pilot, thinking the pilot had been ejected during the crash sequence. I hesitated before admitting it was me. He was surprised and asked me to stand still while he evaluated me. He was looking at my eyes to see if they were both coordinated and on the same horizontal level for a possible head injury. Then he told me to lie down on a stretcher that they were unloading from the fire truck. I refused and then we argued.

I said I wasn't injured and was going to walk back to the ramp. I was in no hurry to face the crowd or my employer, Al Amatuzio, who was in attendance. I didn't know if I had screwed up in front of 90,000 spectators or if I had a malfunction. He finally agreed to let me ride back in the front seat of the emergency truck to the triage room in the Formula One hangar. Dad was there waiting for me shaking like a leaf, thinking the worst.

The Medevac Helicopter

The National Guard evac helicopter had been launched from mid-field to the crash site to transport me downtown to St. Mary's Hospital. It arrived just after the first emergency responders and had then been waived off in another big cloud of dust. The grandstand crowd assumed there was nothing left of me to pick up.

The doctors looked me over for 15 minutes, and now I was beginning to feel some pain. I had a separated shoulder and a badly-sprained left ankle. There was a hole in the Kevlar fire wall where I had stood on the brakes when I hit the ground. It appeared that I pushed my foot through the firewall with a lot of adrenalin.

Al Kramer stuck his nose in the door and said, "Danny, don't worry. It wasn't your fault." That really gave me a sense of relief. From his vantage point in the air behind me, it looked like Don Beck had run me into the ground.

The doctors told me to go home and rest. I spend the afternoon recuperating in an RV camper belonging to Capt. Max Jones, one of my AGS instructors near the pits. It was a week later before I was able to put any weight on the ankle.

General Edsall Calls Cheryl

General Floyd Edsall, the race director, called my wife in Placerville, California and told her I was involved in a little incident and was okay. She was on the road 15 minutes later en route to Reno, some two hours away.

She caught up with me at the hotel that evening while I was watching my alma mater, Arizona State tie UCLA in a football game on TV. She asked if I had been to the hospital for x-rays and insisted on taking me there. I made her wait until the game was finished. I spent most of the night in Emergency waiting for the doctors to get around to seeing me.

Bittersweet Dreams

The local TV news broadcast was picked up nationally and the whole country got to see me screw up. It had started with a dream as a kid; became a reality with challenges surrounded by risks and success. Now I know why they call it the scatter pylon! I called it a bittersweet dream.

Al Kramer offered me his airplane for the championship race on Sunday but I was in no condition to fly. His offer was a complete surprise due to our conflicts in the past. I had my arm in a sling and a sprained ankle.

The next morning, Phil Barber of the Reno-Gazette Journal, interviewed me as I sat at the entrance to pit row in front of the biplane hangar. He asked if I was going to race again. I told him that slipping in a bathtub didn't mean never taking a bath again. He printed that in the Monday morning paper. Cheryl read it while eating breakfast at the hotel and commented, "Mort, you broke your bathtub."

Stall versus Wake Turbulence?

My initial comment to the FAA inspectors was that I did not know if I had stalled in the turn; encountered wake turbulence; or the control linkage to the ailerons had failed. They reported to the NTSB that the aircraft stalled but this is incorrect. In the video tape, the nose is seen to pitch up as I used full rudder in a 90 degree bank in an attempt to arrest the sink rate. A stall would have caused the nose to drop.

United States Air Racing Association Election

On Saturday evening, hours after the crash, USARA had the annual dinner and election of officers. Since I was not present, they took advantage of the situation and elected me president. Within a few months, I had mediated the bickering between NAG (National Air-racing Group) and USARA and merged the two organizations with the help of Chuck Andrews, the immediate past president.

N301LS on Display

I can't express how much I appreciate the support from Al Amatuzio and AMSOIL after the accident. It was apparent by looking at the video that I had encountered wake turbulence.

The aircraft was placed in storage and a few years later, it was restored for static display and placed in the Hilton Hotel at the Reno McCarran Airport. Baron Hilton and AMSOIL split the $14,000 and I chipped in $2000 to close the deal. The Hilton was later sold and became the Grand Sierra Resort and Casino.

The Reno Hilton   EAA Museum, Oshkosh, WI

It was hung from the ceiling over the pylon bar in the biggest Race and Sports venue in town. Sit at the bar and tell them you were Danny Mortensen and you would get a free drink (my name was on the side of the fuselage). If you were not into betting, you could sit in the Johnny Rockets restaurant while looking at the racer. The hotel changed the decor years later and we moved the Racer to the EAA Museum in Oshkosh, Wisconsin where it now hangs in the Rutan exhibit.

Racing Biplane Class Disbanded

With the loss of the AMSOIL Rutan Racer, the Racing Biplane Class was discontinued as there were no new fast racers under development. Only the Sport Biplane Class remains. Don Beck donated the Sorceress to the Smithsonian. Pat Hines donated Sundancer to the San Diego Air and Space Museum. Al Kramer retired his Cobra and put it on display in his shop, San-Val Aviation at Van Nuys.

October 28, 1983, Back in the Saddle

Eleven days after the accident, I flew a Cessna Citation trip to Saskatchewan, Canada transporting Al Amatuzio and staff.

John Denver

I had met the corporate pilots who flew for John Denver at a flight engineer course I was teaching at John Wayne Airport in Santa Ana, CA. They gave me two backstage passes to his concert and Cheryl and I had the pleasure of meeting him. He was an accomplished pilot himself as well as his father who held a world speed record in the USAF B56 Hustler. I asked him if he would like to try a record attempt in the AMSOIL Rutan Racer and he said, "Absolutely, yes." I thought it would be great publicity for AMSOIL to have some celebrities fly the plane.

Coordination with his office resulted in an October 1983 date for a speed record attempt in New Jersey but with the loss of the ship, it did not happen. It is ironic that he would lose his life in a Rutan VariEze in the Pacific ocean off the Monterey Peninsula several years later.

May 6, 1984, the Smithsonian Air and Space Museum, Washington, DC

I was invited to the Smithsonian Air and Space Museum to make a presentation on the Racer by Walt Boyne, the Director. On the commercial flight there, I was arranging slides for the evening. That night, I finally realized I had something to do with the accident. One slide showed me in the cockpit at sunrise for a test flight the morning of the crash and I looked exhausted. The next slide showed a PBS cameraman filming me and I had a big smile.

Looking back at all the adventures in the AMSOIL Rutan Racer, I must have had nine lives. The ship was a pleasure to fly; a student pilot could have flown it. I confess my test pilot skills were sufficient but my decision-making skills in putting myself in some of these situations were certainly deficient.

In a competitive sport such as air racing, there is risk and the chance that incidents and accidents will happen. Race pilots fly on the edge, and it only takes a small error in judgment or circumstances and the result is a bent airplane or injured pilot, or worse. Since the air races in Reno began some 50 years ago, there have been 21 fatal crashes. It is not a sport to be taken lightly. "Expecting life to treat you well because you are a good person is like expecting an angry bull not to charge because you are a vegetarian" Shari R. Barr.

August 25, 1984, Rickenbacker Airport, Columbus, Ohio

This was my first race after the crash at Reno 11 months earlier. I purchased the Mongoose, Race 91, N911S, from Bill Nagle in Kalamazoo, MI for $15,000 and flew it to Rickenbacker in an hour and a half. I really liked the registration number, 911, because it was the number to call in an emergency and I didn't have to memorize it.

On the race horse start, I let everyone take off ahead of me and then I followed. I was nervous about wake turbulence and my heartbeat was high. I had flown the boss in the Citation a week after the Reno crash with no emotional scars but flying in a race for the first time, I had butterflies.

Looking at the video tape, I'm not even in the picture. I climbed to 400 feet above the other seven racers and finished in second place behind Don Fairbanks in the White Knight. I had a faster airplane but was too wide on the turns watching the others below me. Don finished at 148.454 mph and I was only 3 seconds behind at 147.373 mph. That was the end of the butterflies and I was back in the thick of things at the next race.

August 30, 1984, Pyramid Lake, Nevada

On the return flight to the west coast, I left Elko, Nevada, a refueling stop, for Reno Stead Airport. The weather forecast was 10 knots of headwind. As the flight progressed, the headwind increased to 40 knots with an approaching cold front and I did not have enough fuel to make it safely to Stead. I made a precautionary crosswind landing on a two lane road on the Pyramid Lake Indian Reservation about 30 miles east of Reno.

The only building in sight on the high desert was a church. I parked the Mong on the lee side of the building and tied it to the church. I hitchhiked into Reno, got a motel, and the next morning, bought a five gallon gas can and got a ride back out to the airplane. Still nobody around. Refueled, took off, and landed at Stead where I left the Mong in a hangar for race week some two weeks away.

For once, I had made the right decision. There definitely was not enough fuel to climb and cross the last 8,000 foot mountain range between me and Stead. There is an old saying: Pilots killed on bad weather days are usually buried on sunny days.

September 16, 1984, National Championship Air Races, Reno, Nevada

I broke the qualifying record at 190.34 mph in the Mong but Don Fairbanks and Don Beck also broke the record at 192.37 and 192.04 respectively.

I renamed the Mongoose, the "AMSOIL Pacific Flyer" after making some modifications. Several mechanics inspected the airplane for me. We all missed one item; the nut and bolt securing the throttle housing to the airframe worked itself loose in the championship race.

I sensed a decrease in rpm coming off pylon 4 on the last lap and pulled up high to look over the instrument panel while retarding the throttle. Not seeing any indication of a problem, I pushed the throttle back up and to my surprise, the engine remained in idle. With no power, I did a 180 turn off pylon five back onto Runway 14 and deadsticked in. I had to avoid traffic head-on in reversing course to the closest runway. I shut down the engine and had to wait some 30 minutes before someone realized I had not returned to the ramp. They finally sent a truck to tow me in.

I had made several attempts to pass Don Beck in his Pitts and each time I started to pass, he added power, pulling slightly ahead and then would slow down. He was experiencing elevator flutter with a loose flying wire. If I had not pulled out of the race, I'm sure he would have experienced airframe failure flying the ship at the edge of structural failure. I received a DNF for sixth place.

May 9, 1985, Hank Ogden

I had the pleasure to meet Lt. Henry "Hank" Ogden on several occasions for lunch and would drive him to some of his appointments in Southern California. Hank was one of the crewmembers on "the First World Flight" of the four Douglas Cruisers in 1924. Lowell Thomas wrote the book by the same name.

Although famous for his participation in the first successful circumnavigation of the world, his proudest achievement was serving as a US Army Depot Commander in Ireland during WWII where they repaired damaged military equipment. Hank was a legend for the ages.

September 2, 1985, Championship Air Races, Cleveland Burke Lakefront, Ohio

For many years, I had the fastest airplane but was not the fastest pilot. The Mong was named the "AMSOIL Pacific Flyer" in honor of Wayman and Candy Dunlap who published the Pacific Flyer monthly aviation newspaper. They had a wonderful sense of humor and gave AMSOIL lots of publicity over the years.

In the heat race, I took a bird through the wind screen rounding pylon four. At 200 mph, the wind ripped my goggles off. Throttle to idle with one hand over my eyes and the other on the stick and deadsticked onto the runway, using the entire length. Mike Benoist fashioned an improvised short lexan windscreen that afternoon.

In the championship race, I was following close behind Don Fairbanks who was in the lead. As I rounded pylon five on each lap, I got a vibration and throttled back. The vibration stopped and I accelerated catching up with Don until pylon five on the next lap. I took second place just one second behind Don.

Inspection of the ship showed no deficiencies. Only then did I identify the problem. The cloth helmet I was wearing had straps and fasteners on the exterior to hold a radio headset. The relative wind off pylon five would catch the straps causing a flutter on the helmet which felt like an airframe problem. The new, shortened windscreen placed my head up in the slipstream. The only sure thing about luck is that it will change.

September 15, 1985, Reno National Championship Air Races, Nevada

I finished the race taking third place behind Beck and Fairbanks. The third place prize money was $1,837.50. First place was $1,937.50. This might cover your expenses for the week with hotels for the crew, meals, and entry fees. The biplanes always got the smallest purse amongst the Unlimited, T6, and Formula One Divisions.

Playboy Magazine

A Japanese spectator gave me a copy of Playboy magazine from Japan published a year earlier. There was a collage of air race photos of Reno including the AMSOIL Rutan Racer. I was probably included because I didn't have my pants on (wheel pants, to be politically correct).

Art Scholl

On Sunday, Professor Art Scholl, world-renown aerobatic pilot, had a broken exhaust stud on the Lycoming engine of his Super Chipmunk. We dug through our collection of nuts and bolts and found what he needed.

Two days later while filming a spin scene from his Pitts S-2 camera ship over the Pacific near San Diego for the movie, Top Gun, he did not recover and crashed into the sea. There was an Airworthiness Directive (AD) on the control stick which may not have been complied with, and it is speculated the stick broke rendering the aircraft uncontrollable.

December 17, 1985, Fallon, Nevada

I was ferrying the Mong to Ogden, Utah to have it fitted to a custom trailer for transport. I got freezer burn in the 1.3 hours to Fallon, Nevada from Lincoln, California and spent the night warming up in a hotel in town. The next morning, the temperature was now colder at 15 F on takeoff. With a speed of 150 mph to Elko in 1.5 hours, the wind chill factor was even lower. I had ice form on my nostrils in that open cockpit.

Refueled and departed for Wendover, Utah only to discover it was zero, zero all the way to Salt Lake (fogged in) so I back-tracked to Wells, Nevada where I pushed the Mong into an open hangar and caught the bus back to Sacramento. The heck with this cold weather open-cockpit flying. There was no room in that little Mong for a heater.

February 27, 1986, the Mong Trailer

I finally retrieved the Mong and finished the flight to Ogden. Bob Schaeffer gave me a ride to Wells in his Bellanca and then an escort to Ogden. He asked how fast the Mong could go. I said "210 mph." He took the lead and never looked back. I didn't realize he was asking my cruise speed. I couldn't match his speed or I would have run out of gas. I followed the railroad tracks across the Great Salt Lake alone and landed 30 minutes later.

Two months later, I arrived in Ogden with my pickup. Eldon Lutz, a Formula One race pilot, had built a flatbed trailer for the Mong and I towed it back to Lincoln. The G-meter in the aircraft showed 9 Gs driving Interstate 80. The engine mount developed a crack from the weight of the engine. That was the first and last time I trailered an aircraft!

September 8-14, 1986, National Championship Air Races, Reno, Nevada

I didn't compete this year and I don't remember why.

December 23, 1986, Voyager Aircraft Lands at Edwards AFB, California

On this morning, I rode with Walt and Terry Brubaker to Mojave from Torrance in their Grumman AA5 aircraft to greet Dick Rutan and Jeana Yeager. They were on the round-the-world non-stop unrefueled Voyager aircraft flight. They set a record of 9 days, 3 minutes, 44 seconds. 55,000 people were present at 8:06 a.m. when they landed on the dry lake bed.

Walt's father, Bob, was a volunteer in the Command Post. I had sold 100 large color prints autographed by Dick and Jeana to help raise money for the flight. Later, Bob and I did a presentation to Northrop Grumman employees in Los Angeles about Dick, Jeana, and the Voyager.

September 14, 1987, National Championship
Air Races, Reno, Nevada

I qualified the Mong but got a bad cold and asked Dave Morss to fly the Mong.

December 7, 1987, Mt. Shasta, California

I conducted a number of Biennial Flight Reviews as a flight instructor. One of my customers, Shane Curry, bought a Seneca in Seattle and asked me to give him some IFR and multi-engine training on the flight back. The anti-ice was not working but ice was not forecast that night.

Approaching Mt. Shasta, we inadvertently entered a thunderstorm and then began picking up light ice and beautiful St. Elmo discharges on the windscreen. I queried the center controller, rather upset that we were in this situation to which he replied he was not painting anything on his radar. We managed to pass through with no further difficulty.

September 13, 1988, National Championship
Air Races, Reno, Nevada

We had just installed a new Lycoming IO-360 engine which was not yet broken in and I asked Dave Morss to fly again. I told Dave to not run full throttle; just fast enough to get into the Gold race and collect some prize money for me to offset the cost of the new $25,000 engine. He didn't follow instructions and ran hard in the heat race, overheating the new engine, and then dropped out. The DNF put him in the Bronze race and a lot less money. I was upset and never asked him fly for me again.

September 17, 1989, National Championship
Air Races, Reno, Nevada

Worked all year on some improvements for more speed and discovered I was now going slower. I took third place behind Tom Aberle and Sam Maxwell. Hard to believe but nothing exciting happened to me at Reno this year.

August 26, 1990, the Mong Annual Inspection

Mike Benoist at Lincoln, California did the annual inspection each year. I did a test hop around the pattern and nearly killed myself on takeoff. We had moved the seat back two inches and it radically changed the center of gravity. The Mong jumped off the runway in 200 feet with the nose almost straight up. I reacted in time by pushing the control stick forward and almost hit the runway on recovery. The aircraft was unstable in this configuration. I managed to nervously get around the pattern and back on the runway. We moved the seat forward to its original position and solved the problem.

The next test flight was uneventful. Mike, concerned about liability with an experimental racer, asked how it flew. I said, "Great." He replied with a smile, "Good, the warranty has expired." I spent $4000 on modifications this year in hopes of going faster and only flew it one hour. The Mong was more expensive to operate on an hourly basis than a four-engine Boeing 747.

September 23, 1990, National Championship
Air Races, Reno, Nevada

My goal since my first race in 1976 was to win Reno and then retire. I had no idea it would take this long to achieve that dream. I had other things on my bucket list and in 1990, I finally checked air racing off the list.

There were faster biplanes but they did not show this year, having been involved in accidents and incidents. I won by attrition. These little taildraggers are a challenge to fly and it is not uncommon for a new owner/pilot to experience loss of control on takeoff or landing and damage their airplane.

I ferried the Mong over the Sierras on September 16 and noticed a 20 lb. drop in oil pressure en route. Made me a little nervous because there was nothing but mountains below me. I couldn't find anything wrong after landing at Reno Stead airport.

On my qualifying run the next day, the oil pressure line to the gauge in the cockpit broke. The line had developed a pinhole leak. I didn't notice anything until landing. My feet were slipping off the now well-oiled rudder/brake pedals.

On shut down, I discovered the entire fuselage, inside and out, was covered with synthetic oil. It took three of us the entire day to clean up the mess and install a new oil line. If I had petroleum oil in the engine, I'm sure it would have seized at some point. AMSOIL automobile tests back in Superior, Wisconsin had shown an engine drained of synthetic would continue to run for at least 30 minutes longer than petroleum oils.

I qualified the fastest at 188.873 mph, some 4 mph faster than Sam Maxwell in a Pitts. I won the Gold on Sunday at 192.278 mph. Maxwell finished at 184.758 mph; a difference of 14 seconds.

I taxied back to the ramp, shut down, and Peggy Dwelle, a fellow racer, met me at the airplane and gave me a big kiss on the cheek and a hug. I took the traditional victory ride in the big white convertible down the flight line with dad and my son, Tye, age 8. They were so proud of me and I really enjoyed sharing that experience with them. First place prize money was $4000.

I immediately posted a little yellow "For Sale" sign on the
Mong in the hangar. A single seat airplane is not practical for a

family. I had purchased a 1953 Cessna 180B from Joe Stancil Jr. in Placerville, California to accommodate Cheryl and the kids. It was time to move on.

For Sale

May 17, 1991, San Carlos, California

I flew 48 minutes to the San Carlos Airport from Loomis to meet with Capt. Bob Norris and his crew at Flight Simulation to discuss business. We had partnered to develop CATS computer testing for the FAA.

The direct crosswinds at San Carlos were fierce and it took me several attempts to finally get the C180 on the ground. As I taxied up to the FBO, all the employees were standing in the windows holding up large white cardboard signs with scoring just like the Olympics. My average score was 7. They had taken bets that I would give up and not land. I had to use my superpowers one more time.

September 15, 1991, National Championship Air Races, Reno, Nevada

I had retired from racing and sold the Mong to Ken Ueno. When he called from Japan inquiring about the ship, I increased the price to $35K from $30K. He didn't quibble over the price and I realized I could have said $40,000. He said he would buy and I asked if he wanted to see the aircraft first. He said "No."

He arrived in Reno three weeks before the race and called from the Peppermill Casino downtown. When I arrived, there were about 15 Japanese waiting for me in the lobby. Ken introduced himself and his pit crew and friends and then handed me a Safeway grocery bag with $35,000 in one hundred dollar bills.

Oh great. I wouldn't make it out of that dark parking lot alive. I asked the group to accompany me to my truck. The next morning, I made the rounds to a number of banks making deposits of less than $10,000 to avoid an IRS audit.

Over the next few days, Ken and I would fly my Cessna 180 taildragger out in the high desert at low level to get him some experience flying in ground contact at 35 feet. We picked out some Joshua trees for pylons for practice. He was no stranger to biplanes. Ken flew airshows in Japan in a two-place Pitts.

Ken won the race on Sunday at 193.268 mph; 3 mph faster than I flew the year before. I was not surprised. He was less than 30 years of age and had the reflexes of a younger man.

I was 46 when I won and was not as sharp physically. He proved that at the Circus Circus Casino which was his sponsor. On a tour of the casino, they invited him to play all the games. He was able to nail the Whac-A-Mole every time. I tried it and could not hit one of those suckers proving the reflexes of a young pilot were better than an older pilot.

A large number of the investors in Circus Circus are Asians, and they were a big part of the tourist trade in Reno and Las Vegas, which explains why they sponsored Ken. They wanted the publicity.

He is the only foreign pilot to win a championship in Reno since its inception in 1964.

The victory was tainted by a challenge from Earl Allen who claimed Ken passed him on pylon three in an unsafe manner. From my vantage point in the pits, it looked like a legal pass. The contest committee upheld the victory.

Ken and I listen to Paul Poberezny, Chairman of the Contest Committee, and president of the Experimental Aircraft Assn., explain that they ruled in favor on Ken.

The next morning while having breakfast with Ken and his crew, he handed me the first place prize money, $2500, as a bonus for helping him. He shipped the Mong back to Japan and it is now on display in a museum there.

A footnote: Ken's grandfather was on the aeronautical engineering team that designed the wing for the Japanese Zero fighter in WWII.

Having commuted to Reno since 1976 to race, I finally moved there after retiring from racing in 1990. The Reno Air Race Assn. (RARA) was looking for a marketing executive to promote the air races and I volunteered. I had the experience but they didn't want a race pilot to have access to their financial wheeling and dealing. Oh well.

For years, they did not have good press coverage in their major market, Northern California. They had managed to burn their bridges with the press and none of the newspapers or TV stations would send reporters to cover the races.

September 25, 1991, We Lose Don Beck

Don frequently did aerobatics over Lake Tahoe in his Christian Eagle biplane. He had taken a very heavy friend along for a ride which put the aircraft in an unsafe CG condition. He was unable to recover from a spin.

Don was a retired USAF colonel who flew test at Edwards Air Force Base which is only one step below the astronaut corps. He always had the attitude that he was a better pilot than the rest of us and the rules only applied to us; not him.

On one occasion while flying a Formula One Cassutt, he did a victory roll on passing the checkered flag; a rules violation. The Contest Committee grounded him for the remainder of the week at Reno. He then wore a baseball cap with a screw protruding for the rest of the week, implying that he had been screwed.

In spite of this, we all liked Don. He was generous and always had a smile and a kind word. His passing was a shock to the racing community. They say that death is just nature's way of telling you to watch your airspeed.

People ask why we fly; isn't it dangerous? Not any more than driving to the supermarket. Eddie Rickenbacker once said, "Accidents are penalties for motion. Setbacks are penalties for success." Everything we do involves risk. Nobody gets involved in air racing to be rich or famous. We fly and race because we love the excitement and camaraderie. It is the challenge of being really good at something; being better at it than most other pilots.

We can't make anything 100 percent safe. Tony Kanaan, the two-time Indy winner, said "If you make it 100 percent safe and there were no limits to push and no risks to take and nothing at stake, then anybody could drive a race car. And if anybody could do my job, I wouldn't want that job . . . no matter what we do, there will always be accidents that we can't prevent. There will always be risk." To which I would add that I'm not afraid to die. I just don't want to be there when it happens.

September 18, 1993, National Championship Air Races, Reno, Nevada

While attending the races this year as a spectator, I was pulled into the FAA headquarters trailer by inspector Clarence Bohartz and informed that I was guilty of an infraction and I was being issued a written violation. I asked what for and was informed that I was a race pilot on the airport without a race plane. Everyone in the trailer got a big laugh at my expense. After his retirement, Clarence was appointed to the RARA Board of Trustees where he is still active. He was one of the good guys in the FAA.

A few years later while visiting the Reno MGM Grand Hotel and Casino on a trip west, I saw a sign indicating that the air race board was meeting downstairs. I cracked the door open to see who was in attendance and Clarence recognized me. He invited me in to say hello to everyone and tell the story of the crash in 1983. I remarked that I would have preferred to be remembered for winning the Gold in 1990 instead of the accident.

The National Air Race Museum, Sparks, Nevada

For two short years, 1993-94, an air race museum was located in Sparks, Nevada. Ed Maloney, founder of the Air Museum in Chino, CA. was the founder. I was in the museum one day watching the crew hang the H1 Hughes Racer replica from the ceiling when the bracket on the ceiling failed and the Racer came crashing to the floor. The cowl brushed my shoulder and ripped the sleeve off my shirt. I had a black and blue shoulder the next day. An inch closer and it would have killed me. The irony of racing all those years only to die in the museum.

Pylon Racing Seminar, Reno, Nevada

If you would like to fly the pylons, there is a three-day qualification requirement each June for rookies and race pilots who have not competed in the last two years. The biplane class is the least expensive as far as the cost of an aircraft is concerned. You can find a nice little flyable sport biplane in Trade-A-Plane for about $20,000. You will need some tailwheel training with an instructor at your local airport first. For more information, visit:

> www.biplaneracing.org
> www.airrace.org
> www.sportclass.com/training/

Don Fairbanks in the White Knight

Chapter 10

Bill Phelps' Airline Ground Schools (AGS)

Founder Bill Phelps

AGS was founded by Bill Phelps in December 1967 to prep pilots for the FAA Airline Transport Pilot written test. The first class was composed of four fellow C130 Hercules pilots at Southern Air Transport in Oakland, California. where Bill flew as a pilot. Based on feedback, Bill was able to begin assembling a data bank of questions for the next class.

Over the years, 55,000 pilots transitioned through the three day weekend AGS test prep classes in preparation for the captain upgrade or the flight engineer entry level position at the airlines with a 99 percent pass rate. The excellent instructors, all retired captains, were Carl Cox, Max Jones, Carl Kaminski, Floyd Krey, "Cal" Callahan, Bob McGalliard, Les Stillwell, and Bill Phelps. I could listen for hours to their stories of flying in the good ol' days.

July 18, 1984, I Join the Staff

Having attended a three day Flight Engineer test prep class with Capt. Floyd Krey as the instructor, I was invited to join the instructor cadre and was assigned the Southern California market. Until this time, Bill Phelps' had only hired retired captains.

Classes were Friday, Saturday and Sunday. That allowed me to travel to airports in Southern California to put up AGS posters on bulletin boards at FBOs. I could drive to every airport with a flight school or corporate flight department over three days. That paid off with an increase in attendance for only a few gallons of gas.

In 1987, Bill Phelps mentioned he was thinking of retiring and I made an offer for the company. The staff expanded to 50 retired captains after I took control. I was blessed to have some "movers and shakers" like Frank Cowles from United, and Les Leech and Hap Slayden from Eastern on board.

Mac McNicol, Flight Crews Intl. (FCI)

Bill told me to visit Captain Mac at FCI in Los Angeles and introduce myself when I arrived in Southern California. I had only been in his office five minutes and he called the Director of Training at Western Airlines and had set me up for an interview as a B737 classroom instructor. I was flattered but Western only paid $22,000/year and AGS paid a lot more (and I only worked weekends for AGS).

I did the interview as a courtesy to Mac and to my surprise was offered a position. It would have involved a two hour commute from Riverside County and a two hour commute home each evening, where we had just bought a house. Western was later bought by Delta. On reflection, I probably would have retired as a Delta captain which was the usual progression for classroom instructors, but I have no regrets. Aviation has been very good to me.

Rod Machado

It was during my assignment to Southern California that I met Rod Machado; an up-and-coming instructor/speaker/humorist/author at a FAA Safety meeting where we were both speaking. I eventually talked Rod into going to the EAA airshow in Oshkosh, Wisconsin in the early 80s and working out of the AGS booth. He has been a featured attraction at the show ever since.

One afternoon, I stepped into the back of an Oshkosh forum tent where Rod was giving a presentation on IFR procedures and recognized Cliff Robertson, the Hollywood actor and pilot in his own right, next to me. He commented that Rod was pretty good and I asked if he would like to meet him. He said "yes." I walked him up to the podium at the conclusion and introduced him to Rod and his wife, Diane. They both assumed Cliff and I were ol' buddies. It was years later when I confessed to Rod and Diane that I did not know him.

An Evening with Champions

To promote AGS, I started exhibiting at aviation trade shows. The EAA at Oshkosh, is the biggest air show in the world with crowds of 800,000 and as many as 14,000 airplanes in one week. I would do several forums each year and noticed that on Sunday evening before the official start of the show on Monday, the Theatre in the Woods was empty. It seats 3,500 people and many a show is "standing room only." My forum tent only held 200. I got a bright idea.

I approached EAA management with a proposal to do a show entitled, "An Evening with Champions" with air race personalities to entertain the approximately 25,000 campers in the woods. They liked the idea and use Sunday night to work all the bugs out of the electronics. I served at Master of Ceremonies for some 30 years and now have turned that honor over to my son, Tye (who does a much better job of it than I ever did).

KFOX 93.5 FM, Redondo Beach, CA

I got another great idea on how to market AGS classes using the radio. KFOX on the pier at Redondo Beach had a talk show format and I organized a 30 minute gig on Friday mornings called "Aviation Showcase." I had a list of famous aviation people that I wanted to meet and interview. If they couldn't come into the studio, I would do the interview by phone.

Roland Sperry was my co-host who had that Texas drawl which is so popular. He flew in WWII and was an announcer at the local air shows. We did 87 programs and we taped each one. The program ended when I bought AGS from Bill Phelps in 1987 and moved to Sacramento. Roland had a tendency to exaggerate his WWII experiences which later got him into trouble with the Flying Tigers Assn.

Southern California has more famous aviation personalities than anywhere else in the world. We could have gone on for years and never run out of people to interview. California is a "Who's Who" of aviation.

Brooke Knapp and Danny

Left to right: Roland Sperry, Rod Machado,
& Danny Mortensen at KFOX.

Bob McCaffery and Danny

Col. Steve Ritchie

Don Downie

Tony Levier

LTC Roland B. Scott

Cmdr. Randy
Cunningham

Roland Sperry, Rod
Machado, and Danny

Howie Keefe   Danny

Christmas 1986

Roland and I hosted an aviation event at the John Wayne Airport with some 30 authors and artists. It was a wine and cheese party where folks could buy Christmas presents from the exhibitors. Rod Machado was working a table with me when a good-looking gal walked up. It was Diane Titterington, another former air traffic controller and pilot. Rod was smitten and the two were married a year later. She says she has him almost trained now.

Experimental Aircraft Association, Oshkosh, Wisconsin

Let me tell you about retired Captain Bill Barnhart. He was the EAA preacher at the little chapel on the airport. I would attend the nondenominational service on Sunday almost every year. He had an amazing gift of being able to communicate to the parishioners with his extemporaneous sermons connecting the Lord and aviation. The most inspiring sermon was "Christ, the Navigator" and I suggested to him that he needed to put it to pen and paper. Sadly, Bill passed on in 2003 and his smile and his stories are lost to the ages.

June 17, 1987, Bill Phelps Retires

When Bill decided to retire, I bought AGS. The classes were streamlined from three days to two days. I had figured out where AGS was deficient in a changing market and made the course correction. In the first year, AGS grossed over $800,000 easily recouping the $80,000 cash I paid for the company.

Super CFI Refresher Clinics

New products and networking are important to a company and its longevity. I added a national Super CFI Refresher Clinic approved by the FAA with some of the best aviation instructors and educators and gave AOPA (Aircraft Owners & Pilots Assn.) a run for their money with Wally Funk, Irv Jasinski, Col. Steve Ritchie, Dr. Jerry

Cockrell, Chas Harrell, Dr. Gary Ferris, Captain Bob Norris, Rod Machado, etc.) Their resumes would take several pages. We averaged 25 - 30 flight instructors each month around the West Coast and did some big, annual programs for state aeronautics departments (Montana, Alaska and Arkansas) with over 150 flight instructors at each one. What a pleasure to work with these professionals.

The Aviation Speakers Bureau

I envisioned an Aviation Speakers Bureau but was too busy to bring it to fruition. I sold the concept to the talented and vivacious Diane Titterington, who was married to Rod Machado and she turned it into a blockbuster operation.

Simulator Training

We also had a full-blown simulator in our offices in Rancho Cordova, California until relocating to Reno, Nevada in 1990.

The Aviation Career Workshops

AGS also offered the Aviation Career Workshops around the western US with experts from various airlines on subjects pertinent to airline hiring with a star-studded cast. This was first presented in

1988 as the Airline Hiring Expo. We did one a month and averaged about 100 attendees at each event.

1988, Capt. Bob Norris and Flight Simulation, San Carlos, California

AGS entered into a rewarding business relationship with Bob and Flight Simulation at the San Carlos airport. Bob was a United pilot and attended one of my Aviation Career Workshops in Phoenix and became a featured speaker on the program.

We went on to found several other business ventures including the Super CFI Refresher Clinics nationwide and CATS FAA computer testing. Bob and his wife, Dee, and their sons, Bruce and Craig, are all pilots and were involved in the business ventures.

Captain Ray Cloutier

Ray joined AGS as a part-time instructor shortly after I bought the business. He had flown for a number of airlines and actually flew crop dusters for Delta Airlines in the early years. He was the Turbojet Systems instructor for Sierra Academy in Oakland, CA where we first met.

I sent Ray around the world several times to teach the Airline Transport Pilot and Flight Engineer test prep courses. His longest trip was Manila when Philippine Airlines went on strike. The pilots union paid for 400 pilots to attend our ATP course for their FAA certificates. Ray managed to train all of them in three weeks. Ray was also involved in the Aviation Career Workshops.

The most exotic location was Mongolia where he taught a dispatcher course for me at their national airline office. He was always available on short notice to pick up a class assignment. Ray was a mentor, a business partner, and confidant. His friendship, humor and business experience are sorely missed.

The Aviation Career and Interview Manual

Bob Norris and I co-authored a book to help pilots with their airline job search. We sold over 10,000 copies. I would do a briefing on the job market to my AGS classes and wrote a monthly column for In-Flight Magazine on airline jobs. This lead to an annual forum at the EAA airshow in Oshkosh, which I still do today. Bob conducted over 4,000 pilot interviews for United Airlines and was well-qualified on the subject.

October 9, 1989, the Cessna 180B

I bought a C180B taildragger, N4US, from Joe Stancil in Placerville, California. I lived only a block from the airport at the time and racked up several hundred hours over the next 3 years. My only exciting moment in the family aircraft was a flight from Cottonwood, Arizona back to Placerville in May 1990.

I was in some pretty good turbulence with my four year old son, Tye, over the high desert near Barstow and my knees would hit the bottom of the instrument panel. My knee inadvertently knocked the Master electrical switch to OFF. Glancing at the fuel gauges, I was shocked to see them on empty. I nearly had a heart attack and started looking for an emergency landing spot in the desert below before realizing what had happened. I turned on the Master, restoring electrics and continued on.

March 26, 1990, B747 Ground School

My old college buddy, Paul Christensen, flew for ARAMCO in Saudi Arabia. He tried for years to entice me to join him but I was determined to win the air races in Reno first. Poor decision-making on my part. Paul left for Southwest Airlines after 10 years in the Saudi desert with one million in his pocket. He is now a retired airline captain.

Paul offered me a spot in a Dalfort B747 class in Dallas, Texas. He and Dave Lewis, another Southwest captain, had put together a class and had one slot left. They were thinking of leaving Southwest for an international carrier and wanted to pad their resumes. Class was taught by A&P mechanics and their approach to performance calculations left something to be desired.

September 1, 1990, AGS Moves to Reno, Nevada

By moving 10 miles across the state line, I was able to escape the bureaucracy and over-regulation. California is a nice place if you are an orange. Nevada does not have a state income tax.

Reno is the "biggest little city in the world". During the week, locals could get dinner and a show at John Ascauga's Nugget in Sparks for $10. You could get anywhere in town in less than 15 minutes.

The scenery was spectacular. We bought a house in 1991 on the south slope of Peavine Mountain looking down on Reno. Reno Stead Airport is an old Air Force Base on the north side of the mountain some 14 miles from downtown. We could watch and hear the Unlimited Racers inbound from over downtown on their approach to Stead for the start of their races.

A popular colloquium with the locals: They say that Reno is so close to hell that you can see Sparks (Nevada). In reality, Reno is great place to live and raise a family. I miss the smell of the sagebrush and the cool winds off the Sierras in the mornings.

I had a tiedown spot on the ramp at Stead Airport. One winter morning, I was planning to fly to Sacramento but the C180 was covered in frost. The sun was shining with clear skies but the outside air temperature was below freezing. You need a clean airplane wing to develop lift.

Without thinking of the consequences, I taxied from my tie-down spot on the ramp to the Aviation Classics hangar and hosed off the airplane to get rid of the frost. The water instantly turned to ice. Boy, was I embarrassed. I then drove the two hours to Sacramento. It took several days for the ice to melt off the airplane.

An interesting thing about mountain flying: when the winds were calm at Stead, the winds over the Sierras would be strong, and vice versa. Night flying was easy. Climb above the highest peaks and stay over Interstate 80 with the headlights on the cars to show the way through the mountains. Only one problem with that. If you encountered cloud cover in the dark, you lose the headlights below. Option - Follow the general heading for 30 minutes; then start a descent, or make a 180 turn and go back to VFR conditions.

October 5, 1992, Sold the Cessna 180

A doctor at Kaiser Permanente in Napa, California saw my beautiful airplane and offered me so much money for it, I sold it. I had paid $20,000 and he offered $50,000. I only had it three years and I still miss that airplane. Today, a C180 lists in Trade-A-Plane for $80,000–$120,000.

1994, Great American Airways, Reno, Nevada

I got a call from Great American, a charter airline in Reno. Their one and only dispatcher had just died of a heart attack and they needed someone part-time to oversee their flight followers. They operated seven DC9s and MD80s. The job lasted nearly two years until I discovered they were cheating on maintenance. They had two sets of logbooks on each aircraft. I asked what was going on and was told my services were no longer needed. The FAA shut them down in 1997 for maintenance violations.

November 5, 1994, Sierra Academy of Aeronautics, Oakland, California

Ray Cloutier at Sierra Academy called me on a Friday afternoon. Their aircraft dispatcher instructor had died of a heart attack on his honeymoon. Could I teach their B727 dispatcher class starting on Monday? They had 12 international students. I was teaching the ATP/Dispatcher test prep classes at AGS but I didn't have a dispatcher certificate. I did have an Airline Transport Pilot and ground instructor certificates which was good enough for the FAA.

Ray explained the lesson plans were on the shelf and I agreed to meet him at the Oakland International Airport on Sunday. To our surprise, there were no lesson plans. The instructor had left nothing in writing. It was a challenge each night preparing for class the next day. At the end of the 12-week class, all the students passed their FAA checkrides. I then took my dispatcher checkride with inspector Bryan Ashley at the Oakland FAA Flight Standards District Office (FSDO) on January 19, 1994.

Skip Everett, president of Sierra, then asked if I would teach the next class. They had hired an instructor but wanted me to oversee the program one more time. The instructor was totally incompetent and I was told to fire him three weeks into the program.

We had a 30-year-old machinist in class, Joe Hendricks, with a private pilot instrument certificate who was really sharp. I hired him to student teach the next class, and I observed. He went on to teach for several years before moving on to Southwest Airlines.

Sandra Cea replaced Joe as the dispatch instructor. By now, I had shortened the class to six weeks and changed to a current production aircraft, the B737-300. Sandra was outstanding and is now a dispatch supervisor and Designated Aircraft Dispatch Examiner (DADE) at Virgin America in San Francisco.

Sierra Academy was housed in the historic hotel on the east side of the airport. My tiny office was actually a former bathroom in the favorite suite of Amelia Earhart. The hotel was also haunted. Late at night you could hear voices and footsteps when no one else was in the building.

All this time I was commuting home to Reno on weekends. During the week, I was a guest at the home of Bob Norris and his lovely wife, Dee in Redwood City. I am forever grateful for their hospitality and friendship.

Bryan Ashley was too busy at the FAA to continue administering dispatch checkrides and called me in Reno asking if I would like to serve as a DADE (Designated Aircraft Dispatcher Examiner) for the FAA. It was a lucrative and enjoyable assignment that lasted 14 years. I gave over 1,000 check rides during that time.

September 3, 1996, The Move to Cincinnati, Ohio

One of my AGS instructors, Jack Vyhnalek, was in the Training Department at DHL Airways in Cincinnati. He asked if I was interested in a training position at DHL and I decided to move the family east. The Cincinnati International Airport is actually located across the Ohio River in Kentucky.

I called the Louisville FAA FSDO and asked if they needed an examiner in Kentucky but they didn't have a dispatch school in the state. It seemed a logical place for a school with all the airlines and corporations headquartered in the area: DHL and Comair in Cincinnati; UPS in Louisville; Emory Air Freight and PSA in Dayton; Executive Jet Management at Lunken; Republic Airlines in Indianapolis, and NetJets and AirNet in Columbus. I wanted to continue administering dispatch checkrides for $250 per person so I wrote a Training Course Outline for a new dispatch school under AGS and submitted a request to the FAA.

About seven months later, the Louisville FSDO approved the request. The first class of three students was taught by John Burrows, a fellow dispatcher. I asked the FAA to conduct the checkrides but they didn't have an inspector with a dispatch certificate in the Louisville office. I suggested I be re-appointed and they sent two inspectors to observe me conducting the checkrides. One was from the Miami FSDO and had the required dispatch certificate. Captain Gerry Milburn, a retired chief pilot from Delta, out of the Louisville, Kentucky, FSDO, was assigned to me as the FAA Principal Operations Inspector. All three students passed and I was back in business as an examiner. The school really took off and we averaged 15 students per class.

Aircraft Dispatcher Distance Learning

People don't have six weeks in their busy lives to attend a school. I saw the need for a shortened course and we were subsequently approved for a two week Distance Learning Course by Gerry

Milburn. Gerry was great to work with. The innovative short course proved very successful.

We had several requirements for the students to complete before arriving for class. It was based on the honor system and we soon discovered that we needed some safeguards to insure the students actually did the pre-study. For one, we required them to be familiar with reading aviation weather (METARs and TAFs). The instructors were spending too much time in class teaching this because the students were arriving unprepared.

I came up with a solution. For those who did not hold at least a FAA private pilot certificate, they must present a passing score from the FAA computer test for private pilots (PAR) in addition to the FAA computer test for dispatchers (ADX). We provided the self-study materials. That solved the problem and the students were better prepared for class, and the FAA oral/practical checkride.

This was so successful that we felt we could shorten the face time in the classroom to six days. Again, the FAA bought off on the concept, and AGS was the first six day program in the country and again very successful.

Becky Perrin

One of my fellow instructors at DHL was Gary Perrin, who was married to a wonderfully talented girl by the name of Becky. I was in need of an office manager for AGS since I was busy full-time at DHL and Gary mentioned his wife was available. She was absolutely fabulous. When they moved to Florida, I discovered that it took two people to replace her. I am forever grateful for the time and energy she provided while managing AGS for me.

Foreign Students and Dispatcher Training

The dispatcher course began attracting foreign students. David Chung of Flight Trans in Seoul, South Korea, became an agent for us and over the years, sent hundreds of students. He would provide some initial training in Seoul and then send them well-prepared for our program.

We also had a large contingent of Saudi students but these were a challenge. They believed everything they need to know can be found in one book—the Koran. We would mail them five or six books to pre-study before arriving and they might read one. They would deliberately fail the Private Pilot or the Dispatcher FAA computer test so they could stay longer in the US and party. They refused to adapt to our daytime schedule and would stay up all night drinking, smoking, and chasing women (but never studying).

Finally, when their fathers, who controlled the money, said "Enough, come home," they would then try to bribe us to give them their certificate, or claim a family member was dying and they must return immediately (with a certificate). We would explain to them that an emergency on their part was not an emergency on our part. They were welcome to return at a later date for another class.

I had one Middle East airline manager offer me $50,000 to take the Airline Transport Pilot written exam for him. I turned him down. Our grads represented AGS worldwide and our reputation was our "stock in trade."

FAA Computer Testing

AGS was a FAA written testing center in Rancho Cordova, CA since the 1970s. All aviation certificates required a written test. The FAA was soliciting bids to computerize their testing. Bob Norris and I took a shot at it. Bob brought in an investor to fund the project and we subsequently received FAA approval nationwide for CATS (Computerized Aviation Testing Service). After opening an AGS office in Florence, KY in 1995, we became a FAA computer testing center again.

In 2008, we had a Korean student retake the computer test for her Airframe & Powerplant mechanic certificate seven times. In 2010, the local FAA FSDO wanted to see copies of her tests in a routine audit, and the office staff had misfiled them. Unable to locate them resulted in a loss of our testing service.

I had relied on the staff to do their jobs as an absentee owner working full-time for the airline. Annual FAA and CATS audits prior to this showed no discrepancies. The staff was worried they might lose their jobs and was not comfortable with the FAA inspectors. The FAA sensed their uneasiness and assumed they were covering up something.

I brought in Trish Porciello from the DHL/ASTAR Training Department to audit the records. She discovered the two employees were involved in a cover-up and had not been maintaining records as required. She informed me that they were not truthful with her or me. I couldn't fire them because there would be nobody to run the business in my absence. I began to look at options.

I was the president and had to take responsibility for their actions. We had a requirement for our dispatcher students to take both the Private Pilot and the Aircraft Dispatcher computer exams. The FAA began an unethical telephone campaign to the other testing centers in the district to not test any AGS students. The FAA would not put it in writing because what they were doing was illegal. The FAA was trying to close down AGS.

For several months, I would drive the foreign students to other cities to test before our class started. This was a big inconvenience and I decided to sell AGS and retire. Then the FAA began a voice campaign to other businesses to not buy AGS. Luckily, a local company, Flamingo Air at Lunken Airport, stepped forward with the courage to not listen to the local FAA.

It only takes one or two FAA inspectors in a district office to ruin the reputation of the entire FSDO. When inspectors go on a personal vendetta, it is to the detriment of that office. Now I knew how Bill Paynter felt at Union Flights in Sacramento years earlier.

Anyone who sets his goals high is bound to have a certain number of failures. I'm reminded of the story of Babe Ruth who set a record for the number of home runs he hit. We tend to forget he also set a record for strikeouts. He didn't let that worry him. He just kept on swinging for the fences.

I hired an excellent aviation attorney, Jerry Eichenberger in Dublin, Ohio to defend me on numerous charges. When the FAA takes action against an individual, they list as many possible viola-tions hoping one will stick. Their letter of investigation was inten-tionally vague. Initially, I had no idea what they were talking about.

This was the only time in the long history of AGS that we were involved in any kind of legal action. It cost me $10,000 and I had to surrender all of my FAA certificates for a period of two years at which time I could reapply for them. If I wanted to continue fighting the FAA, it would have cost me at least $50,000. It made sense to simply acquiesce to the allegations. I retook the dispatcher, ground instruc-tor, and private pilot checkrides and passed.

I am reminded of a quote from Charles Dickens. "Reflect upon your present blessings, of which every man has many—not on your past misfortunes, of which all men have some."

March 10, 2001, the Cessna 150, call sign N150MC

My son, Tye, was now 15 years of age and wanted to fly. I bought him a C150 instrument trainer with a STOL (Short Takeoff and Landing) kit and arranged for Carl Krueger, one of our DHL instructors to work with him. We based the C150 at the Gene Snyder Airport in Falmouth, Kentucky about 30 air miles south of Cincinnati. We then built a $45,000 hangar from our AGS profits for our $22,000 airplane.

It is logical to the IRS that an aviation company should have an airplane. It is also logical that a company would then be able to depreciate said airplane. Over the years, I depreciated every airplane for advertising, training and transportation. All you need is an avia-tion-connected business and the airplane pays for itself.

May 6, 2009, the Cabin Waco, VKS-7, call sign NC29372

We eventually sold the C150 and bought a classic 1940 biplane from a retired American Airlines chief pilot, David Graben, in Dallas for $65,000. It needed a lot of work but it had dual controls and wide landing gear with a 240 hp Continental W670M radial engine. It had not flown in 10 years so I ferried it to Radial Engines in Guthrie,

OK for some work. The radio was useless because of interference from the unshielded sparkplug lines. They looked at it and determined it really needed a new engine, so I left it there and flew home commercially from Oklahoma City.

After the new engine installation, we did a partial restoration and repainted it. It is simply gorgeous and attracts crowds everywhere. After retiring in 2010, I now have an aviation consulting company, Fearless Froggy Aviation, Inc. to which the ship is registered for tax and liability purposes.

AGS Scholarships

My business plan involved exhibiting at aviation trade shows such as Women in Aviation and the National Business Aircraft Association (NBAA). I would award one or two dispatcher training scholarships at each event. AGS has helped hundreds of students who otherwise could not afford the training. By 2010, the total amount of awards was more than $60,000.

July 22, 2010, AGS Sold to Flamingo Air

I retired from the airline in June and sold AGS to Capt. David MacDonald and Sharon McGee at Flamingo Air at Lunken Airport in Cincinnati. I remain involved as a consultant and part-time instructor.

My success in business and life is because of hard work. I had two full-time jobs with AGS and DHL/ASTAR Air Cargo. I worked seven days a week, rarely taking a day off. The only place where success comes before work is in the dictionary. I shared my secret to success with people and watched them fail in their endeavors because they were not willing to make the commitment.

Kemmon Wilson, Founder of the Holiday Inns and Words of Wisdom

Folks are more willing to accept ideas if you tell them someone else said it first. I found this posted on the wall at the Wilson Air Center, an FBO in Memphis where we taught dispatch classes to Fedex employees.

1. Work only half a day - makes no difference which half - it can be the first 12 hours or the last 12.
2. Work is the master key that opens the door to all opportunities.

3. Mental attitude plays a more important rule in a person's success or failure than mental capacity.
4. We all climb the ladder one step at a time.
5. Two ways to get to the top of an oak tree. Plant an acorn and sit on it or climb the tree.
6. Do not be afraid of taking a chance. Remember that a broken watch is exactly right at least twice a day every 24 hours.
7. The secret of happiness is not doing what I like but in liking what I do.
8. Eliminate from your vocabulary the words, "I don't think I can" and substitute, "I know I can."
9. In evaluating a career, put opportunity ahead of security.
10. Remember that success requires half luck and half brains.
11. A person has to take risks to succeed.
12. People who take pains need to be paid more than they get paid for, and never get paid for anything more than they do.
13. No job is too hard as long as you are smart enough to find someone else to do it for you.
14. Opportunity comes often. It knocks as long as you have an ear trained to hear it, and eye trained to see it, a hand trained to grasp it, and a head trained to use it.
15. You cannot procrastinate—in two days, tomorrow will be yesterday.
16. Sell your wristwatch and buy an alarm clock.
17. A successful person realizes his personal responsibility for self-motivation. He starts himself because he possesses the key to his own ignition switch.
18. Do not worry. You cannot change the past, but you could ruin the present by worrying over the future. Half the things we worry about never happen, and the other half are going to happen anyway. So why worry?
19. It is not how much you have, but how much you enjoy that makes happiness.
20. Believe in God and obey the 10 commandments.

Aircraft Dispatcher Opportunities

The aircraft dispatcher is the highest paying job on the ground at an airline. A senior dispatcher makes half of what a senior captain at a major airline makes. Dispatcher salaries with 15 - 20 years seniority are about $100,000/year. If you are going to work eight hours a day, you might as well work in a profession that pays the most for a day's work.

You will need to accrue a minimum of two years' experience at a commuter airline first. Starting salaries for new dispatchers are about $25,000 per year with automatic upgrades each year. Some dispatcher offices are unionized.

I think working as a dispatcher is better than flying the line. You are home every night for dinner. You don't live out of a suitcase. With my airline ID and my dispatcher certificate, I could go to the terminal and request a jump seat authorization form from any airline. The gate agent would take it to the cockpit for approval by the captain. I was never denied access except when the fight was full. The captain would generally offer the jump seat on the flight deck or a seat in first class if one were available.

You could go anywhere in the world for free. I would catch the 4:30 p.m. Delta flight from Cincinnati nonstop to Paris and go Christmas shopping on a weekend in December. It's a wonderful life.

Working in dispatch is a backdoor to the airline cockpit if you are a commercial pilot. On bad weather days, management is looking over your shoulder to ensure a smooth operation. You get to know senior management. They usually ask why you are not flying for them when they discover you are an aviator. It is easier to be selected for a pilot slot from within the company as opposed to interviewing off the street.

If interested in an airline dispatcher career, I suggest you contact AGS at: 1-800-824-4170 or www.flamingoair.net or www.agschools. com.

Chapter 11

DHL Airways

September 3, 1996, Working For an Airline

I joined the training department at DHL at the Greater Cincinnati International Airport in 1996. The training department was in disarray and they needed someone with my training expertise to help upgrade the program.

Pete Blessing, the Director of Training, along with the instructor cadre, was impressed with my 15 minute presentation on B727 Weight and Balance and thus began a wonderful 14 year airline career. I wish I had kept a diary of all the characters and events. It would have made a great book.

Tell someone you work at an airline and he will tell you how much better your airline is compared to his. As with any corporate operation, there are always some mismanagement problems but overall, the employees make good decisions. Your people make the difference in success and failure.

Deutsche Post of Germany

Deutsche Post acquired a 22.5 percent interest in DHL in 1998 gradually increasing to 100 percent in 2001–2002. In July 2003, they decided that they did not want to own airplanes and sold the airline to John Dasburg, the former CEO of Northwest Airlines, and his associates, renaming it ASTAR AIR CARGO. We became a subcontractor to DHL.

Airline Perks

The ASTAR pilots would bid their flying lines so that they could have their weekends at home. The flights on Friday nights were usually the last flight until Monday evening. The company had hotel rooms booked for the entire week but the rooms were not used if the crew was local.

I would check with the crew flying to JFK. If they were not using the room, I would ride the jumpseat with them and spend the weekend in New York visiting the museums, etc with a free sleeping room at a very nice hotel. I then rode back with them on Monday evening.

The Software Self-Study Fiasco

The company wanted to improve the classroom training and hired a software company to develop a self-study computer simulation of the flight deck instrumentation at a cost of some $450,000. One of our instructors, Chuck Ross, pointed out that he could do it in-house in PowerPoint and save money.

A contract was written anyway but failed to require the developer to provide the software code. A lot of our man-hours were spent in trying to fix the inconsistencies and the developers finally refused to work on the project anymore. We never implemented the program.

2008, the DHL / UPS Merger

In 2008, DHL announced plans to merge with UPS and terminate its relationship with ASTAR but that plan ultimately failed one year later. UPS came out a winner by taking a portion of the business away from DHL during the negotiations as DHL began sharing its customer database in good faith.

Bonuses

Management had a bonus each year for their managers, but not the employees. There are no secrets with 1,200 employees and 550 pilots. When we found out about our boss getting a $50,000 bonus, we make a big stink about it. The boss didn't do any teaching or curriculum development. It just wasn't fair. We did the work in the trenches. Eventually the program was expanded and all the employees got an annual bonus. I got $4,000 the first year.

The Philadelphia Caper and Other Stories

DHL was our primary customer. One winter evening, the Philly airport was closed due to ice. DHL insisted we fly there anyway since they paid for the fuel. The captain and the dispatcher discussed the situation, and added extra fuel to hold over the Philadelphia airport for an hour, and then return to Cincinnati, the alternate airport on the dispatch release if the airport did not open. Everybody was happy. The captain got paid for flying and management wasn't upset with the dispatcher for canceling the flight. The freight was trucked the next day.

Vip Nath, the dispatch supervisor, got upset with DHL one night, and walked out of the building, telling everyone he quit. He had been there so many years that management forgave him and rewarded him with his retirement and vacation pay.

One of our classroom instructors, John, was in charge of the emergency training including live fire drills and the life raft and life preserver training in the pool. We would borrow the pool for an hour each week at the Holiday Inn for Recurrent Training. He was curious about the dye marker in the survival kit and opened it, tossing it in the pool, and to his surprise, contaminated the pool to a very distinct yellow color. They had to drain the pool and it took them three days to clean it.

We were told we were not welcome at the Holiday Inn anymore. John was relieved of that aspect of training and I was designated the new emergency drill trainer. We needed a pool. I called the Holiday Inn and said I was with Delta Airlines and got the pool.

APU Inoperative

The Minimum Equipment List for the B727 states that an inop Auxiliary Power Unit (APU) must be repaired within 10 days during which time the aircraft can continue to operate. Maintenance repaired the unit but failed to notify Maintenance Control. The item was listed as a Deferred Maintenance Item (DMI) on the dispatch release notifying the dispatchers and pilots, as required.

Unfortunately, the aircraft was operated for several days beyond the drop dead date meaning the aircraft should have been parked until fixed. We call this scenario an AOG (Aircraft On Ground). The FAA, during a routine paperwork audit, discovered the discrepancy and mandated a Letter of Reprimand be placed in the file of each pilot and dispatcher who operated the aircraft during the period beyond the 10 day envelope.

One of the affected captains asked a mechanic buddy why they dropped the ball to which the mechanic replied that they had repaired the APU and returned to service within the 10 day window. The captain asked management to review the paperwork and logbooks showing there was no infraction but the company was not interested in spending man-hours researching the records in storage.

The captain and the mechanic on their day off searched the records in the storage warehouse and found proof that the repair had been made within the allotted time and presented the evidence to the FAA. The FAA rescinded the Letter of Reprimand in all the personnel files, no thanks to management.

Airline Captains

Arguing with an airline captain is like arguing with a motorcycle cop. It's a "no win" situation. As a dispatcher, the only way to manage a captain who wanted to divert to an alternate airport not on his dispatch release, was to simply say, "Captain, understand you are declaring an emergency and diverting to X airport." That usually resolved the situation. He didn't want to declare an emergency and then have to face the chief pilot when he returned; not to mention the paperwork required.

We had one captain who would take his burned out light bulbs from home on trips and replace them in the hotel room for working bulbs. Airline pilots are famous for pinching pennies.

The standing joke was that some captains were so cheap that they would donate their white uniform shirts to Good Will, who would clean them and then put them on the rack for sale. The captains would buy them back for .75 cents which was cheaper than taking them to the cleaners.

Captain "Salty" Roark

One of the original cadre at DHL Airways was Salty Roark, seniority number one. When he reached the mandatory retirement age for a captain, he downgraded to the flight engineer seat on the DC8. Since he knew every nut and bolt on the airplane, there was no reason for him to stay awake in the flight engineer initial training class. He would immediately assume a semi-prone position when class started with his head resting on the back of the soft chair looking at the ceiling (with his eyes closed). One of the pilots taped the electrical schematic to the ceiling over his seat so he could review it without inconveniencing himself.

Salty lives near the old Cincinnati Lunken Airport. He is one of the staunchest opponents to the airport and complains about airport noise, bless his heart. Salty was one of my favorite captains.

Captain Ted Kissel

Ted was another member of the wonderful original cast of characters at DHL. I really enjoyed working with him in the training department; a wonderful sense of humor. Ted and a couple of the instructors went to lunch at the local Chinese buffet. Some two hours later, they were thrown out by the owner yelling, "You eat too much . . . you go now."

Captain Paul Waters

Paul was on the DC8 and a simulator instructor in the training department. He always had a kind word and a big smile. His help on international flying subjects was much appreciated. In his off hours, he is a financial consultant and an expert on investments and retirement. Thanks to him, many of the employees have a great retirement fund including me. I told him to invest my funds wherever he personally invested his money. That philosophy worked.

DHL Moves to Wilmington, Ohio

DHL is bigger worldwide than Fedex and UPS combined. DHL bought Airborne Express (ABX Air), a competitor in Wilmington about 1 1/2 hours north of Cincinnati (CVG). The price was 1.05 billion and included the ownership of the airport, an old Air Force base. DHL decided to combine operations there and would have two airlines to serve the nationwide network. ASTAR left Cincinnati and moved to Wilmington. If one airline went on strike, the other would continue to operate.

The operation fell apart beginning with the first night in 2006. The freight was not getting sorted and distributed to the aircraft on time, if at all, due to a shortage of personnel. ABX Air began to stash freight in various buildings, hiding it from DHL. Some of it was in the warehouses for two weeks instead of guaranteed next day delivery.

The ABX employees did not want ASTAR on the property. ABX airplanes got priority handling from the ABX tower. DHL resorted to bussing prisoners from the local jail to help. Customers were upset with late deliveries and the brand was hurt badly.

The experiment lasted four years and cost DHL hundreds of millions of dollars. DHL finally decided to move the operation back to the Cincinnati International Airport (CVG) in 2009. We (ASTAR) tried to tell Frank Appel, the general Director of Deutsche

Post, that it was not a sound decision to leave the Cincinnati airport in the first place, especially after spending millions to upgrade the facilities at CVG. We could see why the hard-headed Germans had lost two world wars!

Why DHL continued to do business with ABX Air is beyond me. ABX was caught one winter night in Wilmington deicing disabled DC9 and DC8 aircraft that were not flyable (and billing DHL for the work). Deutsch Post donated the Wilmington Airport to the Clinton County Airport Authority when they returned to Cincinnati.

Ted Mallory

We had some great managers. Dasburg brought in General Ted Mallory from Atlanta, a retired B747 captain and former Director of Training at Northwest Airlines (NWA), to run the operation. The general needed a place to stay during the week and heard that I had an empty bedroom in my condo in Wilmington. That arrangement caused some consternation with my boss, the Director of Training, who was concerned that I might be privy to confidential senior management topics. Ted would frequently ask me to drive him as his chauffeur in the evenings as he was on the phone constantly. He was a wonderful man; a true professional and it was my honor to work for him.

He would occasionally ask my opinion about somebody or some procedure or policy. My boss, a director, was an inept, insecure manager with no people skills who did not fly often enough to maintain currency. He once remarked to me that "Everybody hates me" to which I responded, "That's not true, not everyone has met you yet." I couldn't resist it. I got the penalty box for that one.

I would come home to Kentucky on my weekends and stay in the condo during the week. I was able to arrange a four day work-week with 10 hour days. My evenings were spent on the computer in the condo on AGS business and creating PowerPoint presentations which I shared with ASTAR. General Mallory took an interest in what I was doing in the evenings and suggested a number of subjects he thought would be useful for ASTAR and AGS.

At one point, the pilots were threatening a strike, and the general offered me a flight engineer seat if the strike went forward. I appreciated the offer but had no intention of crossing a picket line to get to the flight deck. I explained to him that I did not qualify for a first class medical due to a heart condition.

Jay Herrin

General Mallory brought in Jay Herrin, another retired NWA B747 captain to run the Training Dept. "Jaybird" was a hands-on people-person and very supportive of the employees. He was a gifted manager; one of those people you rarely meet in life that really inspires you; someone you would follow anywhere. He improved the morale and professionalism of the staff.

Eric Bergesen

When Jay left, he was replaced with one of our outstanding young Airbus captains, Eric Bergesen. Eric had a totally different management style. He was well-liked but his office was in complete disarray with papers stacked everywhere. I offered several times to help him with his workload but he was the type that had difficulty delegating his projects. I think management enjoyed overloading him with assignments. Eric was another people-person who was also a pleasure to work with and had a great sense of humor.

Dan McMahon

Captain Dan McMahon was in charge of the ground instructors when I joined in 1996. He was on a medical disability from Delta Airlines and taught the B727. He was another gifted instructor. I worked with him for five years until he regained his medical certificate and returned to flying at Delta.

After he retired, we traveled to Greece together in 2015 to visit my relatives in the village. He had never been there and enjoyed seeing Greece from a different perspective than most tourists. I introduced him to the sister of my grandfather, Mantha Kolymbaris, who was 107 years old. In 2017, both he and his wife accompanied me to Greece for Easter services.

All of my supervisors had a "hands off" management approach. On the days I was not teaching, I was allowed to work unsupervised, creating new PowerPoint programs for the training department. I would identify areas in which we had no materials, do the research, and then put something together where it would sit on the shelf awaiting a request. When I first arrived on the scene, the instructors were using overheads. I brought my AGS aviation video collection to the department which was much appreciated.

Carl Kruger

Carl is a great pilot, instructor, and friend. He left ASTAR before it parked the aircraft and accepted an instructor position with Federal Express in Memphis. Fedex tried to recruit me also but Cheryl didn't want to move to Memphis. The normal Fedex progression was classroom instructor and then a flying position. That philosophy changed and Carl was not able to make the move to the cockpit. He resigned from Fedex (their loss) and is now flying B737s for Allegiant back in Cincinnati.

Joe Spielmann

Joe was in management in the maintenance department. For a short time, he was one of our instructors in the training department. He is also a free-lance A&P mechanic inspector and does the annual inspections on general aviation aircraft, including mine. Joe was a stickler for the rules and was not popular with the Maintenance Vice-President, who bent the rules to suit him and his buddies.

At one point in time, the company was thinking of contracting out the maintenance training and was soliciting bids. Since I owned Airline Ground Schools, I was asked to submit a bid. In reality, DHL had already decided to whom they were going to award the bid -

Boeing, because they were negotiating with them for B737 freighter conversions (which never happened).

Joe invited me to his office when he was opening the bids. I was the low bidder at $1 million but the bid was awarded to Boeing. The company was afraid I would raid the training department for instructors to staff AGS. Joe and I had a good laugh on how things really worked at DHL—the good ol' buddy system.

Neither of us fit in. If you didn't play golf, drink with management, and chase women with them after work, you were an outsider. I was invited once or twice to join their group but declined. The wife had dinner waiting every night, and I would rather be home with the family. Joe is in management now with General Electric overseeing production of their aircraft engines.

Training Department Observations

The training department is the best place to work at an airline. It was like working at a country club. I got into trouble with management for saying this in the cafeteria in front of employees one day from other departments. I qualified the statement in the future by adding, "If it were not for management." If there is a strike or lay-off, the instructors are the last ones to go. When I taught recurrent class each week to the pilots, I could see how much they had aged from the previous year due to flying on the backside of the clock. Flying at night for seven straight days is fatiguing.

The training department was in a separate building from headquarters for several years. Whenever I went to the headquarters building, I carried a large stack of papers and walked fast as if in a hurry to avoid being tasked with additional duties. It was a self-defense mechanism.

We moved the training department several times to other locations. Each time we moved, huge amounts of training materials, slides, office supplies, etc. were tossed out in the dumpsters. I became a professional dumpster diver after work and would find new binders, office supplies, systems manuals, etc. which I would take to Airline Ground Schools.

My initial assignment was the B727 Systems but spent most of my time teaching Basic Indoc and Initial training to new pilots, System Safety, Recurrent training, Security, International Operations, Human Factors and Crew Resource Management, Dispatcher training, Air Traffic Control, Controlled Flight Into Terrain, Instrument Procedures, Recurrent, Meteorology, Operations Specifications, Regulations, MELs/CDLs, Aerodynamics, Publications, Navigation, Airport Analysis, Company Manuals, and Emergency Equipment. The line pilots served as simulator instructors and did not like classroom teaching. We ground instructors were referred to as SME's (Subject Matter Experts). I enjoyed it.

Captain Upgrade Training

We created a New Captain training program. Just because you were now a captain based on seniority didn't mean you had leadership or management skills (or common sense). This was a two-day program to address the new issues they would face from the left seat. It was well-received and we eventually expanded it to include all the captains no matter how long they had been flying as Pilot-In-Command. It was a rewarding interchange with the pilots and they much appreciated it.

Teaching Schedule

My teaching schedule was usually one day a week when I would entertain the pilots with the Recurrent Subjects required each year. Whenever we had a class of new hires, I would teach the required subjects for three straight weeks. I would add humor to make the presentations more enjoyable. A favorite pastime was to slip a funny slide into one of the presentations just before another instructor taught a class to the chagrin of the instructor and the enjoyment of the pilots.

When I was not teaching, I was tasked with developing/updating PowerPoint presentations on current and anticipated future subjects. I had negotiated an agreement with Pete Blessing, the Director of Operations, that any materials I created could be shared with dispatcher training at Airline Ground Schools. Any materials I created at AGS would be shared with DHL/ASTAR.

I horse-traded with other airlines for PowerPoint and videos too. When I joined DHL, they had seven old videos on the shelf and no PowerPoint. When I retired, we had over 300 videos on the shelf to supplement the training program plus 400 of my PowerPoint presentations that I had created on every imaginable aviation subject.

Night Flying

Flying at night is not conducive to longevity. The pilots would fly a seven day schedule and then have seven days off. It was tough each week readjusting from a day schedule at home with the family back to flying at night.

It was difficult the first day back from a weekend while working as an air traffic controller. We would start our five day week with a late afternoon or evening shift and then finish the week with an early morning shift, giving us a long three day break. The first night back, we all had trouble staying awake. I would sometimes take a nap at the end of my last day in the break room before attempting to drive or fly home.

Fatigue was insidious and no one was immune. Riding the jumpseat around the country at night, I would watch the pilots take a cat nap in the cockpit, one at a time. One captain remarked, "Don't let me wake up and find you guys sleeping." The instrument approach at the destination in the early morning hours could be a challenge in weather, having been flying all night. My hat is off to all of them. We never had an accident.

In the hub, we had a dark room with very comfortable recliners for the pilots to sleep while the boxes were sorted and redistributed to the appropriate aircraft. If someone inadvertently turned on the lights, everyone would scatter like cockroaches.

No Accidents but Several Incidents

Lima, Peru: We had a DC8 enroute to the states out of Santiago, Chile, with a full load of cargo. The load planners in Santiago miscalculated the weights and gave the numbers to the crew in kilograms instead of pounds (1 kilo equals 2.2 lbs). The captain asked them to verify "pounds, not kilograms." After takeoff, the crew had trouble controlling the airplane and declared an emergency, landing in Panama. The load planners were fired. They were prosecuted and jailed by the Peruvian government for attempted murder. A little harsh by U.S. standards.

Cincinnati: We had a B727 that was loaded nose-heavy and used the entire runway in Cincinnati before rotating for takeoff due to an incorrect weight and balance computation by the Load Planning Department. Captain Chuck Duty was the captain and returned for a landing while dumping fuel to get down to a safe landing weight. He demanded all the containers be removed and re-weighed. The load planner was fired.

This wasn't the first time. We had a DC8 out of San Francisco leave a wake trail across the bay trying to get the nose up on takeoff. Captain Dick Prescott was the Pilot-In-Command (PIC) who related the story to me. Another Load Planner was fired for incompetence. The FAA stepped in and insisted we add safeguards to the system to prevent any further occurrences.

Amarillo: A B727 flight out Cincinnati for Phoenix had several MEL (Minimum Equipment List) discrepancies in the fuel system before departure. A fuel gauge was not working in one tank. Then a fuel valve failed during refueling. The mechanic explained that he had wired the valve "open" and discussed the issue with the captain.

An hour after departure, the crew had been rerouted by ATC and did not have the opportunity to do the usual fuel score evaluation. A little later, the captain noticed one wing was lower and the autopilot had not corrected the situation. He trimmed the 727 but an hour later, the situation had reoccurred. Then he noticed the fuel gauge appeared to be working.

It was time to call Dispatch and connect to Maintenance Control to discuss it. The call was dropped during the discussion due to atmospherics. Maintenance and dispatch had no idea that a mechanic had done something to the airplane. The mechanic had not informed them of his repair.

The aircraft was now seriously not flying level. The crew declared an emergency to ATC and was directed to the nearest airport, Amarillo. Not having approach charts for that airport, a Fedex crew on the frequency supplied the necessary information since we didn't service that airport.

On landing, the pilots used 15 degrees of flaps instead of the usual 30 flaps, and full rudder to maintain runway centerline. It was a difficult landing at a higher landing speed. On shut down and inspection, it was discovered the mechanic had wired the fuel valve in a "closed" position and that tank and associated engine were very close to flame out. The mechanic was fired.

JFK, New York: A night departure out of JFK with a B727 experienced an engine failure just after takeoff. The crew declared an emergency and was radar-vectored over Long Island back to the runway. The crew immediately began dumping fuel to get down to a safe landing weight as per company procedure. Jet fuel will take the paint off cars. US Senator D'Amato was one of the unfortunate victims under the flight path.

Departure Control (radar) failed to tell the tower in a timely fashion that we were coming back with only two engines. The tower put a British B747 into position on the runway and could not get them clear in time for our arrival. Our crew did a two-engine go-around and another lap around Long Island dumping fuel.

On landing, a main landing gear collapsed and now we had a disabled aircraft on the runway for 13 hours, totally disrupting

Loaded on a truck

arrivals into New York. Thankfully, there were no serious injuries to the five employees on board.

There was an AD (Airworthiness Directive) from the FAA to all Boeing operators that a crack had occurred on a Delta 727 several years earlier within the wing that was not visible to a walk-around inspection. That aircraft experienced a gear collapse. A FAA recommendation was made to x-ray all 727s but was not mandatory. Shortly after this incident, DHL did x-ray all the birds. Our aircraft was written off by the insurance company due to its age and flight time on the airframe.

Saltio, Mexico: We had a daily B727 flight to Saltio arriving each morning at 7 a.m. when the control tower opened. On this particular morning, the airport was shrouded in fog. The alternate airport was listed in the dispatch release as San Antonio, TX—the airport of departure.

The crew called dispatch to discuss amending the dispatch release to nearby Monterey, Mexico but lost radio contact with dispatch before completing the amendment. An amendment requires time and initials from the dispatcher in Cincinnati on the recording tape to be legal.

The crew, having flown throughout the night and now fatigued, didn't realize the radio transmission was incomplete. They should have returned to San Antonio but went to Monterey. Nobody at Monterey was expecting them.

The company did not think to self-disclose what had happened to the FAA. When the FAA learned later, they insisted the company place the flight crew on a three day suspension without pay. A self-disclosure usually results in no FAA action other than "don't do it again."

Mexico City, Mexico: Our DC8 crew was cleared for takeoff. It was dark with light rain. A fully loaded Air France B777 made a wrong turn leaving its gate to taxi and incurred on the active runway. The flight engineer, Scott McDorman, saw the B777 lights ahead and yelled, "Abort!" The captain, Steve Norris, veered off the active runway into the mud to avoid a collision. The DC8 was stuck deep in mud for a day. The freight missed the sort here in Cincinnati that night. Subsequently, whenever the Air France captain arrived at JFK, he dropped off a case of champagne for our DC8 captain with his sincerest apologies.

Lexington, KY: The captain, out of Florida enroute to Cincinnati at night, was circumnavigating thunderstorms. He assumed thunderstorms were in progress at Cincinnati as he neared CVG and elected to land short at Lexington nearby.

Earlier, while taxing out in Miami, one of the crew members had cut his finger and pulled a Band-Aid from the first aid kit. The Minimum Equipment List requires the first aid kit to be replenished by maintenance before the next flight and a mechanic signature in the logbook. The flight is grounded until this is accomplished. The crew didn't think of this when they diverted. There was no DHL mechanic in Lexington. A mechanic drove from CVG to Lexington to correct the situation. The irony was that Cincinnati was open - no storms.

The freight missed the sort and was not delivered the next day to the customers around the country. If the freight is not delivered on time, the customer does not pay for it. The captain should have called dispatch before diverting to discuss an update to the weather in Cincinnati.

While we had our share of misadventures at the airline, we were no different from any other airline. It was a great place to work in spite of our problems. For the most part, the people were terrific. It is said that 90 percent of the problems at a company are caused by 10 percent of the employees. We were not immune to this axiom.

Cincinnati: The control tower takes the hourly weather observation at CVG. On this particular night, light icing was present. Our General Operations Manual allows operations in light icing conditions with the usual precautions such as deicing of the aircraft on the ground before departure. The tower was reporting moderate icing conditions, however.

All departures were halted for two hours before the chief pilot's office thought to call the tower cab to discuss the situation. The Tower controller had failed to place a minus sign in front of the icing symbol representing LIGHT icing when he took the observation. The lesson here is that we must be advocates for our operation. If we do not agree with the weather report, call the observer and discuss it. Ask for a new observation.

The Simulator Sessions

I would occasionally observe the pilots in the simulator going through their practice drills. Most were very good and professional in their approach to the challenges of dealing with both routine and emergency maneuvers. Each year, a different set of requirements were dictated by the training syllabus.

I watched one captain who was not good at delegating the workload and used poor decision-making skills. Later I asked the sim instructor why the captain was not written up for these failures in Crew Resource Management (CRM) and was told it was not one of the items being reviewed and graded that year. I was dumbfounded to discover that we had holes in our training philosophy. That was one captain I made a point to never ride with on the jumpseat.

I wasn't the only one. The union and the company created a short list of pilots who refused to ride with each other for various reasons. The dispatchers had their own unofficial black list of a few captains they did not respect!

Special Ed

We had a few pilots who were "weak" and would do anything to avoid annual recurrent training. Ed would call in "sick" on the first day of recurrent training which would force the company to reschedule him to a later class date. Sometimes these pilots would be out on sick leave for months with feigned illnesses backed up with excuses from a doctor.

The gals in the Training Records office, Trish, Ellen, and Sandy, named him "Special Ed" because of his "no show" each year for Recurrent class. No airline is immune from this abuse. It was expensive to do one-on-one training. Ed's luck ran out when he was arrested by the police in a city park for some infraction. We never saw him again.

FAR 121.652 Landing Weather Minimums: IFR...

Having served eight years as a controller, I was the "go-to" guy in the company on air traffic control questions. Shortly after joining the staff, I discovered that the company was misinterpreting one of the regulations. In discussing FAR 121.652 with the chief pilots, I was unable to convince them that they were wrong.

As a result, I wrote to Legal at FAA Headquarters (commonly referred to as the Puzzle Palace) in Washington, DC for an opinion on behalf of Airline Ground Schools. Their letter confirmed my interpretation.

The reg says that landing minimums for new captains with less than 100 hours in the left seat must increase their personal minimums by 100 feet and 1/2 SM, and in the case of an alternate airport, the landing minimums can never be less than 300 feet (ceiling) and 1 mile (visibility).

The company thought this was a pre-flight requirement and did not apply once the flight was enroute. I showed the FAA letter to the Chief Pilots and the General Operations Manual was changed to reflect the correct interpretation. The three Chief Pilots were appreciative of my approach to solving this without bringing any embarrassment to them in the eyes of the local FAA office or the company pilots which had not noticed the discrepancy.

Scott Adams and Dilbert

I was out of work for several months with a serious illness. While in the hospital recovering from emergency surgery, my boss visited and brought a Dilbert calendar to cheer me up. When I returned to work, I put it on my desk. There were so many appropriate cartoons to our management staff that other employees would make a point to stop by the cubicle each day to read the daily offering.

Some of those would then appear on bulletin boards throughout the company and I was told to stop posting them (which I wasn't doing). When I explained to the boss that he had given it to me, he said, "Ya, but I thought you were dying." I sent an email to Scott

Adams, the creator of Dilbert, and he said he was going to use it in a future cartoon.

I didn't have enough sick leave accrued to cover my six weeks of recovery but Sandy, our administrative assistant in the Training Department, on behalf of the company, continued to pay me as if I was at work every day. It truly was a great place to work.

PowerPoint

DHL was transitioning from overheads to PowerPoint presentations but would not spend any money to train us on how to create PowerPoint. I pointed out that a one day training session for our instructors would be cost effective as opposed to everyone individually wasting time trying to figure it out on their own.

No dice. There was lots of wasted man-hours and frustration as a result with no standardization between instructors. Some of stuff being created was just awful. Our manager got a bigger bonus at the end of the year if he didn't use all the dollars in his budget. Same was true for travel and off-site training seminars—didn't happen. Ground instructors had to work with what they brought to the table when they signed on.

The Divorce

One of our captains was going through a bitter divorce. His vindictive wife called the FAA and said he was suicidal just to get even. The FAA revoked his flying privileges requiring him to see a psychologist. He was declared "fit to fly" and he was the only pilot amongst our 550 pilots who was certified on paper as mentally competent.

The Christmas Party

Picture this: a Christmas party at the home of one of our pilots. The host was demonstrating his quick draw technique to the crowd and accidently discharged the weapon. He shot one of our pilots who managed to survive. Since it happened off company property and the wounded pilot did not file any charges, nothing became of it except a loss of pride and a great sense of embarrassment to our weapons expert.

The DC8 Door Trainer

We had a FAA requirement to open and close the door each year in annual recurrent training. We did not have the luxury of the training department located on the airport where we could walk out on the ramp to do this plus there wasn't always a DC8 available. We had an Airbus A300 and a Boeing 727 door trainer but no Douglas DC8 door trainer.

The solution was to find a derelict DC8 and cut out the door assembly, rebuild it into a working door trainer, and place it in the training department. I found an abandoned DC8 in South America and arranged to have the door cut out and brought back on one of our DC8s. We smuggled it past customs in Los Angeles by simply not mentioning it was on board and then delivered it to a machine shop for repair and restoration. Quotes from the industry were $75,000 or more for a new door trainer. I got this one for a total of $14,000 when all was said and done. Never did get a "thank you" from management.

Customs and Cigars

One of our popular captains, Scott MacGregor, flew the New York - Caribbean routes frequently. He would bring on board as many as 50 boxes of Cuban cigars on each return flight for resale but would forget to declare them to customs. This went on for years. One morning, he was discovered and Customs fined him $100,000. Scott was allowed to continue flying. He smiles when he tells the story which seems to indicate he came out ahead on the deal. He told me recently that it paid for the college education for all of his kids even with the fine thrown in.

The company had a rule that no alcohol was allowed on the property or the aircraft. The crews including the chief pilots routinely brought back duty free booze on overseas trips!

Operating Certificate

The company was the only freight airline that had FAA authority to not only operate as a Supplemental Part 121 air carrier (charters) but also operate as a Flag and/or Domestic flight. The company got the FAA approval to enable them to take advantage of the pilots by reclassifying the flights to the advantage of the company. The rest rules were different for each type of operation and as a result, the pay was different.

Pet Peeve

One of my pet peeves about passenger flying involves the emergency briefing you receive from the flight attendants (FAs). My solution to people not paying attention to the FA spiel is instruct everyone to sit in a circle at the gate in the terminal and receive the briefing, like you did in elementary school. A written test would be administered and if you didn't pass it, you would not be allowed on the airplane.

Management and Leadership

We had some incompetent people in leadership positions. I was determined to outlast them. The company thought that since you were a captain, you could lead a department. There is nothing farther from the truth. What are the most common complaints of workers about their bosses? In a survey of several thousand employees, the top ten were:

Arbitrariness
Arrogance
Failure to show appreciation or give credit
Failure to see the other person's point of view
Failure to size up employees correctly
Lack of leadership
Lack of frankness and sincerity

Failure to delegate responsibility
Indecision
Bias—letting emotions rule reason.
Plus: lack of courtesy, sarcasm, jealousy, nervousness, and frequent loss of temper.

We had one Director of Operations (DO), David Reeve, who stood at the door to the ramp one night and handed out pencils to the pilots with the DHL logo as a Christmas present. No bonus, no Christmas turkeys—just pencils. This really upset the pilots. The DO had no idea how much his attempt at camaraderie had backfired. This was an example of how management was out of touch with the troops.

Corporate Buzz Words

We had some favorite terms we used internally to describe working within the corporation:

> **BLAME-STORMING**: Sitting around in a group, discussing why a deadline was missed or a project failed, and who was responsible.

> **SEAGULL MANAGER**: A manager who flies in, makes a lot of noise, eats the food, craps on everything, and then leaves.

> **CUBE FARM:** An office filled with cubicles.

> **PRAIRIE DOGGING**: When someone yells or drops something loudly in a cube farm, and people's heads pop up over the walls to see what's going on.

> **MOUSE POTATO:** The on-line, wired generation's answer to the couch potato.

SITCOMs: (Single Income, Two Children, Oppressive Mortgage). What yuppies turn into when they have children and one of them stops working to stay home with the kids.

STARTER MARRIAGE: A short-lived first marriage that ends in divorce with no kids, no property, and no regrets.

STRESS PUPPY: A person who seems to thrive on being stressed out and whiny.

SWIPED OUT: An ATM or credit card that has been rendered useless because the magnetic strip is worn away from extensive use. We had several captains who had to use their personal credit cards to buy fuel for the jet to get home because dispatch forgot to arrange billing.

ASSMOSIS: The process by which some people seem to absorb success and advancement by kissing up to the boss rather than working hard.

IRRITAINMENT: Entertainment and media spectacles that are annoying but you find yourself unable to stop watching them in the break room. CNN, later known as the Clinton News Network, was one of them.

PERCUSSIVE MAINTENANCE: The fine art of whacking the heck out of an electronic device to get it to work again.

SALMON DAY: The experience of spending an entire day swimming upstream only to get screwed and die in the end.

ADMINISPHERE: The rarified organizational layers beginning just above the rank and file. Decisions that fall from the Adminisphere are profoundly inappropriate or irrelevant to the problems they were designed to solve.

404: Someone who's clueless. From the Worldwide Web error message, "404 not found," meaning that the requested document could not be located.

Retirement

In 2010, with 14 years of service, I retired. AGS had a contract with Turkish Airlines to provide Dispatcher Recurrent Training in Istanbul. Vip Nath, the former DHL dispatch supervisor, and Capt. Ray Cloutier conducted the training on a recurrent basis for me.

Turkish Airlines asked for a copy of my PowerPoint presentations which I sent to them on a CD. Included was a draft security presentation I was preparing for my AGS dispatch classes. I used the FAA template but deleted the confidential material proprietary to the FAA. The FAA became aware of the security presentation and assumed it was their original presentation. ASTAR was forced to suspend me. Rather than fight the system, I resigned and took my retirement funds to the bank.

June 1, 2012, ASTAR Ceases Operations

DHL abruptly terminated its contract with ASTAR and the aircraft were sent to the bone yard in Kingman, Arizona. DHL wanted ASTAR to park the old, expensive-to-operate gas-guzzlin' fleet of B727s, A300s, and DC8s and replace them with newer B737s with fuel-conscious CFM engines. John Dasburg, the CEO, had a golden parachute of $25 million if DHL canceled the contract. I can only assume that the CEO found it convenient to not acquiesce to the DHL request to spend his money to secure a freighter version of the 737.

Another factor was pilot pay. ASTAR pilots were the envy of the industry. They had the highest salary amongst US carriers. This was an incentive to DHL to cancel the contract and hire less expensive contractor airlines to provide lift.

The pilots refused to renegotiate their salaries to keep their jobs and a great little airline became history. The former employees still refer to DHL affectionately as Dewey, Huey, and Louie airlines.

DC8

B727

A300

Chapter 12

Crew Resource Management (CRM)

History of CRM

CRM started with KLM, the Royal Dutch Airline, after the Tenerife accident in 1977 when two B747s collided in fog on a runway in the Canary Islands. It was the world's worst aviation accident—578 died.

KLM did some soul-searching to uncover the cause of the accident and as a result, developed the first Cockpit Resource Management training course for pilots. Human error was the primary cause but other factors: fog, frequency congestion, a lack of situational awareness, and fatigue were interfaced.

In 1977, near Salt Lake City, Utah; and again in 1978 at Portland, Oregon, United Airlines lost a DC8 and began questioning what they were doing wrong. How could those accidents have been prevented?

In 1980, United, in conjunction with NASA Researchers at Moffett Field in California, introduced CRM in the US. Eventually, it became Crew Resource Management encompassing all the airline employees working with the pilots: dispatchers, flight attendants, mechanics, meteorologists, etc. It has grown worldwide within a larger field of study known as Human Factors.

In the early aviation years, it was man versus nature, solo, single-seat, open-cockpit airplanes with an attitude that the mail must go through. The idea of a captain making all the decisions without any input from two- and three-man crews permeated the cockpit until the eighties. The captain was God and you did not speak to him unless he spoke to you first. As a result, we had a lot of accidents.

Pre-CRM Captains

We had a couple of old captains at DHL who were not crew-oriented. In other words, they were typical pre-CRM types; authoritative; not interested in their co-workers. One morning, one of our copilots reached for the thrust levers and the captain slapped his hand and told him not to touch them. "Everything on this side of the cockpit belongs to me." An investigation followed and the captain was fired for striking a first officer. The irony was that you could shoot a pilot accidently at a Christmas party but you couldn't strike him or you would lose your job at DHL.

Now don't get me wrong. As I said earlier, we had a wonderful cadre of pilots and dispatchers who bought into the CRM concept when it was introduced in the late 1990s at our airline. I was privileged to be involved in the development. One retired United captain teaching for me at Airline Ground Schools, Frank Cowles, was instrumental in the creation of CRM at United and provided much appreciated info and support. CRM eventually became known as Command, Leadership, Resource Management (CLRM) at United.

Each airline customized its program. At American Airlines, it is now known as Human Factors and Safety. At DHL, the CEO did the same and changed CRM to TRM (Team Resource Management) without consulting the staff; another example of a failure to solicit input.

It took us several days to effect the change in our system. I thought Communications Resource Management would have been better and would not have disrupted the organization. After all, communications (or lack thereof) is the biggest part of CRM. Miscommunication has caused many aviation accidents.

Human Factors

We haven't discussed the broader field of Human Factors (HF) under which we find CRM, nor have we addressed motivation, leadership, and fellowship. HF encompasses how people interact with aircraft, each other, and the aviation system as a whole to avoid, trap, and manage errors. It includes Standard Operating Procedures (SOPs), equipment design, checklist usage, automation, safety programs, and aircrew and aircraft support training.

The goal is to improve safety and operational effectiveness. Human Factors is a science that focuses on physical and psychological aspects and on how people interact with machines, policies, and the operational support structure. The medical profession, fire fighters, police, etc. have adopted it.

Star Trek

Are you are a fan of the original Star Trek series which ran from 1966 to 1969? Captain James T. Kirk knew all, saw all, and did all solo. The cast of characters were there to support him. He made all the decisions without any input from the crew (pre-CRM).

Gene Roddenberry was the creator who flew in WWII and then for PanAm but his dream was to write scripts for Hollywood. He quit the airline but couldn't find sufficient work after creating the first Star Trek series. He then joined the Los Angeles Police Department. Several years passed and along came CRM in 1980. It was there that he discovered CRM as it permeated from the airlines to law enforcement.

He created the new series with Captain Jean-Luc Picard which ran from 1987 to 1994. Picard was an intellectual; an explorer of history and knowledge. He practiced CRM and used all of the talent of his crew to arrive at decisions. The two captains had totally different leadership styles. If you had to choose which team you would like to be on, I'm sure you would pick the latter series.

Threat and Error Management

CRM has progressed over the years through several levels of sophistication. The latest development involves Threat and Error Management (TEM). It provides the enabling behaviors that pilots and dispatchers need to manage risk. First, identify the risk. Second, eliminate or reduce the risk to an acceptable level. Third, assess resources and crew capabilities. Last, apply appropriate resources and capabilities to maximize the safety margin.

The Cleveland Scenario

Here is a historical event. Is this approach safe or unsafe for an airline pilot? Picture an ILS approach to Runway 05.

Visibility 1 3/4 miles with light snow.
Runway contaminated with snow.
Braking action reported good by a corporate King Air pilot.
Wind 330 degrees at 18 knots gusting 28 knots.
First officer is flying (300 hours in the aircraft).
Captain has 5000 hours in the aircraft.

Most airline pilots would accept this level of risk but only with the captain flying the aircraft. Now throw in the fact that ATC reported braking action from the previous arriving aircraft, an MD88 airliner, as poor, and most professional pilots would divert to the alternate airport. In fact, this passenger jet ran off the end of the runway in Cleveland, Ohio.

What is a threat?

It is something that will impact safety of flight, but originates outside the cockpit (or dispatch office) environment. Risk comes from threats. Valid strategies for dealing with threats are 1) change airports, 2) change runways, 3) hold waiting for the snow to stop, 4) ask for the runway to be plowed, 5) solicit more information on braking action, 6) require the captain to fly the aircraft in these conditions.

While technical proficiency is the foundation of safe flight operations, crews are tasked with responsibility for safe, legal, and reliable operations as a result of their decision-making. Technical proficiency is rarely the cause of aviation incidents and accidents. Traditional airline training and evaluation for years emphasized the technical aspects of pilot proficiency. Stick and rudder skills are necessary but analysis of NASA research and NTSB accident data shows incidents and accidents are more likely caused by ineffective crew management than poor pilot skills.

Proper decision-making is a result of Situational Awareness (SA): what has happened in the past, what is happening now, and what will happen in the future. SA is dependent on the free and open flow of communication. In summary, SA, decision-making, and communication are dependent on teamwork, leadership, and followship skills on the flight deck.

I recommend some wonderful Human Factors books by Robert L. Helmreich, H. Clayton Foushee, Earl L. Wiener, David C. Nagel, Jerry Harvey, and Tony Kern if you wish to learn more about CRM.

The Core CRM philosophy is based on six concepts common to most airlines and ATC:

1. COMMUNICATION

Effective CRM begins with effective communication. It is the verbal and non-verbal exchange of information between people. Message content is relayed in approximately the following proportions:
Body language 55 percent, Tone 38 percent, and Words 7 percent.

<u>All Team Members should:</u>

* Listen actively.
* Provide and accept timely, constructive feedback.
* Use standard terminology and phraseology.
* Communicate changes or expected changes to automation, systems, flight status, etc.
* Gain the attention of team members before communicating.
* Balance communications with operational demand and priorities.
* Communicate information and decisions clearly.

<u>Captains/Supervisors should:</u>

* Create a climate for free and open communications (set the tone).
* Establish and reinforce two-way communication channels with other team members.

* Brief operational requirements and expectations in a timely fashion and inform the team of unexpected contingencies.
* Ensure that tasks and responsibilities are understood among the team.

First Officers should:

* Offer or assert their perspective when safety and/or efficiency would be enhanced.

Dispatchers and Controllers should:

* Give and receive thorough briefings.

2. TEAM COORDINATION

This is the action and strategies used by team members to facilitate teamwork in a coherent and unified manner by setting the tone, prioritizing, managing, and monitoring.

All Team Members should:

* Acknowledge changes in operational status to automated Systems as outlined in the company manuals.
* Provide timely input to accomplish tasks, and assert experience and knowledge when needed.
* Support other team members.
* Monitor how the team is setting the tone, prioritizing, and managing.
* Provide constructive feedback and accept team critique without becoming defensive.
* Acknowledge mistakes and/or limitations promptly.
* Resolve disparities in interpretation, priority, and techniques.

<u>Captains/Supervisors should:</u>

*   Create an environment for open communication through briefings and soliciting input.
*   Coordinate and facilitate the completion of normal and abnormal tasks, clearly stating responsibilities of each team member.
*   Coordinate aircraft and situation monitoring.
*   Assigns tasks according to team member duty position and workload (considering experience and skill levels).

<u>First Officers should:</u>

*   Inform the captain of task progress and status at the appropriate time.
*   Ask for clarification of roles and responsibilities when uncertain.
*   Be assertive as appropriate for the situation.
*   Be ready to assume situational leadership when directed.

<u>Dispatchers and Controllers should:</u>

*   Provide current information, in a timely manner, to other team members to facilitate their decision-making.

Note: The secret of success in communication is to be able to disagree without being disagreeable.

3. PLANNING

The selection of actions and strategies to meet current and future requirements. Team members will fulfill their role as effective planners by consistently anticipating operational requirements.

<u>All Team Members should:</u>

* Plan ahead to accomplish future tasks in an efficient manner.
* Adapt to changes and factors that affect the current or future flight status.
* Plan, brief, and prioritize team tasks.
* Plan and brief the modes and configurations of automation to be used.
* Communicate changes to or deviations from the plan.

<u>Captains/Supervisors should:</u>

* Focus the team's attention on upcoming requirements and demands.

<u>First Officers should:</u>

* Call the team's attention to anticipated requirements which have not been addressed.
* Ask for clarification when plans are not clear.

<u>Dispatchers and Controllers should:</u>

* Focus attention on limitations of the flight crew due to weather and maintenance factors.

4. WORKLOAD MANAGEMENT

A strategy that allows for timely and appropriate completion of all operational tasks. Workload demands change significantly during flight operations. Proper management ensures that the team takes advantage of periods of low workload to reduce later periods of high workload.

Proper workload management ensures that no single team member becomes overloaded.

Team members will fulfill the role as effective workload managers by consistently utilizing individual and team skills to manage time-critical tasks when situational demands force the team to prioritize in this order: Prioritize, Assign or Assume tasks, and Manage time.

All Team Members should:

* Prioritize individual tasks according to situational demands and published procedures.
* Prepare for times of high workload during low workload periods.
* Recognize and communicate when becoming overloaded.
* Use the appropriate automation level for reducing workload.

Captains/Supervisors should:

* Prioritize and assign team tasks according to operational demands and given situations.
* Manage time to accomplish tasks and make decisions when becoming overloaded.

First Officers should:

* Be available for other tasks when another team member's workload is high.
* Suggest priorities that will enhance the completion of critical tasks.

Dispatchers and Controllers should:

* Recognize that time requirements may vary from task to task, and allocate accordingly.

* Allow time for handling possible abnormal and irregular operations.
* Be proactive.
* Use all time productively.

5. SITUATIONAL AWARENESS

Situational awareness (SA) is knowing where you are, what's going on around you, and projecting future needs; essential to effective decision-making. The team maintains effective SA by constantly refocusing their attention to assimilate key elements of the environment necessary to support the selection of appropriate courses of action. Think outside the box.

<u>All Team Members should:</u>

* Ensure distractions do not detract from overall team SA.
* Alert team members when added vigilance or attention may be necessary.
* Recognize and inform other team members when your or their individual SA is in doubt. (Ask questions to validate)
* Maintain an awareness of the automation/systems modes and capabilities selected by the team or automatically initiated by the aircraft (mode awareness).
* Recognize when automation is becoming a detriment to SA and use a more appropriate level of automation.

<u>Captains/Supervisors should:</u>

* Brief or initiate strategies for handling distractions.
* Assume/assign monitoring duties for specific requirements.

First Officers should:

* Share information to enhance team awareness.
* If SA is in doubt, suggest priorities or courses of action.
* If SA remains in doubt, become more assertive.

Dispatchers and Controllers should:

* Be alert to other team members around you: crew schedulers, mechanics, dispatchers, and controllers.

6. DECISION-MAKING

Effective decision-making is the use of a systematic approach to consistently determine the best course of action in response to a given set of circumstances. This involves information management and choosing amongst alternatives.

Team members will fulfill their roles as effective decision-makers by consistently selecting a safe and effective course of action, while utilizing all available resources appropriate to present or anticipated conditions.

All Team Members should:

* Look for multiple clues to identify the problem.
* State symptoms, not conclusions, when initially identifying the problem.
* Proactively contribute to the research of options.
* Consider time restraints when selecting a course of action.
* Consider operational priorities and risk when selecting a course of action.
* Review assumptions before committing to a course of action.
* Re-evaluate decisions as conditions warrant.

<u>Captains/Supervisors should:</u>

* Initiate and direct research and information gathering efforts.
* Select options and make decisions in accordance with manuals and operational guidelines.

<u>First Officers should:</u>

* Proactively contribute to the selection of a course of action.

<u>Dispatchers and Controllers should:</u>

* Invite participation of appropriate departments.
* Exercise authority.

SUMMARY: An effective captain establishes the team concept early based on: boundaries, norms, and authority.

There are always a few that refuse to cooperate with their fellow employees. We had one or two captains like that. One DC8 captain pushed the flight envelope and was fired. He was too high on approach and should have gone around for another attempt. Instead, he decided to slip the four-engine heavy jet by cross-controls to lose altitude and scared the crew. They stated, "Go around" emphatically but to no avail. It was an unauthorized procedure and had never been done before. DHL, the manufacturer, and the FAA did not approve.

We have SOPs for operating aircraft to prevent incidents and accidents. Deviations are expected and the regulations make allowances for them but aircraft designers and regulatory authorities can't think of every possible circumstance. The regulation FAR 91.3 gives the Pilot-In-Command the authority to deviate from the regs to the extent required if an in-flight emergency requires immediate action. Pilots may find it necessary to alter or skip a SOP for safety reasons.

Sometimes we make decisions that, at the time, seem prudent but on reflection, may have been just laziness, expedient, or simply an error in judgment. We are human; not perfect. We make mistakes. Training is designed to prevent or mitigate them before they become harmful. As professionals, we train to minimize deviations and to recover from those that do occur. Here is an example:

July 19, 1989, United Airlines Flight 232

The most successful example of Command Leadership Resource Management (CLRM) was UA Flight 232 which diverted to Sioux City, Iowa after their number two engine exploded on the DC10 tri-jet (see YouTube). I had the honor of introducing both Captain Al Haynes and Captain Denny Fitch at the EAA Theatre in the Woods in Oshkosh, a few years ago as Master of Ceremonies.

Theirs is an amazing story in the annals of aviation history. Some 50 plus crews flew the accident scenario in the simulator later and were not able to reach the airport. The synergism exhibited by the teamwork of the crew was outstanding. The CLRM training at United was credited for the survival of 185 passengers in a seemingly impossible situation.

Judgment

Can we teach judgment? Most of us do not have the luxury of a Judgment 101 class in school. We are not born with it. We learn it by observing human behavior in our leaders, teachers, parents, friends, etc. That reminds me of the saying, "You can be intelligent but not educated. You can be educated but not intelligent. You could be both or neither." Aviation is unforgiving and riddled with lots of examples of poor judgment. As stated earlier, human error is the number one cause of accidents, incidents, and miscommunications.

What is good judgment?

* It is the ability to make a quick decision assuring the best possible outcome.
* It is often a series of evaluations over time that keeps you out of danger.

* It is the intangible components of flying which enhance safety.
* It is the ability to recognize certain risks are involved.
* A safe pilot consistently makes good judgment calls and decisions.

The Rule of Three:

Physical, Equipment, Weather—any one of those can force the cancelation of a flight. It is not unusual to have a "write-up" in a system; sometimes even two squawks in the same system. The "write-up" must be repaired or deferred as per the Minimum Equipment List. If it is deferred, it is called a DMI; Deferred Maintenance Item, and must be repaired within a certain time period. We have redundancy in aircraft systems. Three failures in one system, even on a VFR day, would probably force an AOG (Airplane On Ground) situation until maintenance fixed the problems. The crew that takes an airplane on a bad weather day or at night with two or three MELs in a specific system is tempting fate. Remember the DHL incident at Amarillo?

December 9, 2004, Atlanta, Georgia

The DHL B727 crew was inbound dodging thunderstorms in the area. They were late in configuring the aircraft for the approach and as a result, were high and fast forcing the aircraft into an unstabilized approach configuration. The correct procedure in a situation like this is to "go around" and then attempt another approach. The captain made an error in judgment and continued the approach. His rate of sink was too high and he hit the runway hard forcing the landing gear up through the wings, and disabling the aircraft on the runway for some 12 hours.

This severely affected arrivals into Atlanta, one of the busiest airports in the country. The crew was sent back to the school house for retraining. The other two flight officers never suggested a 'go around' to the captain. This is an example of a failure of both leadership and followship; both preconditions for good CRM.

A primary tenet of any airline operation is "safe and legal" and the order in which this is accomplished does not matter. You can be safe but not legal, and you can be legal but not safe. The crew in Atlanta broke both rules.

Negotiation with the FAA got this reduced to an incident in spite of the fact the aircraft was a total loss. Note the Landing gear twisted 90 degrees and driven up through the wing.

Another CRM Debacle

Dispatch would prepare the flight plans for the crews. On this particular day, dispatch filed the DC8 flight plan from Cincinnati to Lima, Peru unaware that there were VOR navigation stations in Chile and Ecuador with the same three-letter identifier along the route. They used one which was 500 miles shorter than required for the fuel load.

The crew arrived late and in their rush, did not take time to program the GPS navigation unit until after departure. Later, in flight, they realized they did not have enough fuel to make Lima and had to land short in Panama due to the incorrect data entry in the GPS. The GPS defaulted to the closer, identical VOR identifier and did not match the Inertial Navigation System data.

This effectively demonstrates failure of the following principles of CRM involving communication, team coordination, planning, and workload management. On the plus side, the crew exercised situational awareness and decision-making in dealing with the problem.

The Five Hazardous Attitudes

Embry-Riddle Aeronautical University years ago developed a line of thought for the FAA called the Five Hazardous Attitudes, all related to judgment.

1. Anti-authority

Why should I listen to you? Don't tell me what to do.

Antidote: Follow the rules. They're usually right. This attitude usually is found in people who are nonconformists. They are unreceptive to comments/advice from superiors or subordinates. The rules are for you; not for me for I am gifted and better than you.

2. Impulsivity

Do it quickly.

Antidote: Not so fast. Think first, then act. These people feel the need to do something immediately. Doing something is better than doing nothing. Example: Entering an unusual attitude while descending in a turn, or flying too slow with ice on the wings (Buffalo, New York; Colgan Air flight 3407; February 12, 2009). The pilot reacted incorrectly by pulling back on the controls further exacerbating the situation and stalling the aircraft.

The proper procedure, if one took a moment to think, would be to reduce engine power to idle, roll wings level, reduce back pressure to lower the nose, and then increase power to recover from the descent. Acting on impulse is dangerous as it usually involves uncalculated and irrational actions.

3. Invulnerability

That will never happen to me.

Antidote: It could happen to you. I can think of a number of good pilots who are no longer with us because they took this premise for granted. They compromised vigilance and overlooked certain issues that seem less important. Skipping the checklist or parts thereof is an example. Accidents can happen to anyone.

4. Macho (or Macho-ette)

I can do this.

Antidote: Taking chances is foolish. The pilot who agrees to fly the Atlantic without an autopilot is compromising safety due to fatigue. We have seen pilots who are mission-oriented or gung-ho to help the company but are actually taking an unnecessary risk. This type of individual thinks he is really good but there are a lots of these types who lost this argument.

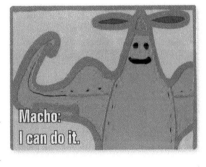

5. Resignation

What's the use? I give up.

Antidote: I'm not helpless. I can make a difference. When operations on the flight deck don't go as planned or confusion arises, it is human nature to blame it on fate. To do so, compromises safety. Pilots must be proactive and reactive. We have SOPs, rules, and regs to help

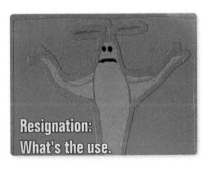

the crew deal with problems. We are in control and not victims of a predetermined destiny.

Pilot Profiles

The characteristics of a pilot in a <u>low accident risk category</u> are: a well-balanced personality; mature; well-controlled; and has a healthy and realistic outlook on life.

The characteristics of a pilot in a <u>high accident risk category</u> are: mentally defective or psychotic; unintelligent, unobservant, inadaptable; disorganized, disoriented, or badly disturbed; has a confused perception of life with a distorted sense of values; exhibits uncontrolled aggression; emotionally unstable; and has anti-social attitudes or criminal tendencies. Luckily, we do not have many of these types in aviation but we do see them in the newspapers every day.

Traits frequently found among people that are considered quite <u>normal</u> are:

* selfish, self-centered.
* highly competitive.
* overconfident, self-assertive.
* irritable and cantankerous.
* people who harbor grudges and grievances.
* always ready with an excuse.
* intolerant and impatient.
* those with marked antagonism and resistance to authority.
* people who are frustrated and discontented.

This is you and me according to the psychologists—normal traits.

Finally, according to transport pilots, the average fighter pilot, despite the sometimes swaggering exterior, is very much capable of such feelings as love, affection, intimacy, and caring. These feelings just don't involve anyone else.

Chapter 13

Safety Management Systems (SMS)

History

SMS is a process for systematically managing safety throughout an organization. It was first developed by Transport Canada after the Air Ontario takeoff accident in Dryden, Ontario on March 10, 1989. It was the most detailed investigation in Canadian history due to 24 fatalities out of 69 on board.

Flight 1363, a Fokker F28 jet was plagued by a number of causal factors including snow and ice on the wings, an inoperative Auxiliary Power Unit, and no available external power at the airport. This led to questionable decision-making. It was an en route stop. If they shut down, they would not be able to restart because of the inop APU. Deicing with engines running was not approved as fumes could enter the aircraft therefore the captain did not deice. The F28 was re-fueled with passengers on board which was prohibited. To disembark the passengers would take too much time and it was snowing. The company was also found to be at fault with nonqualified people in management positions.

The FAA adopted the SMS philosophy and required all US airlines to add the training to their curriculums. ICAO, the International Civil Aviation Organization, mandated SMS training worldwide in 2009.

The FAA taught a three day SMS class for us at ASTAR at a cost of $10,000. Why three days? Government employees travel on Monday, teach Tuesday through Thursday and then travel home on Friday. That allows them a full work week out of the office. Quality suffers when instructors stretch out a program without meaningful dialog and material.

Brad McCool and I reworked the material and taught the class in-house in eight hours for the employees who did not attend the bureaucratic FAA presentation.

System Safety is anticipating and controlling hazards by designing them out of the system—not simply identifying deficiencies after an undesired event. The formula for success involves: 1) identifying and managing hazards, 2) assessing and measuring safety risks, and 3) modifying the management of hazards.

What is a Hazard

A hazard is a condition or circumstance that can lead to physical injury or damage; a danger. A risk is the consequence of a hazard, measured in forms of severity and likelihood; an uncertainty.

Principles of Risk Management

The first principle is to accept no unnecessary risk. A risk is unacceptable if it carries no commensurate return in terms of benefits or opportunities.

The second principle is to make risk decisions at the appropriate level. The appropriate decision-maker is one who has the authority to allocate resources needed to reduce or eliminate the risk and implement the necessary controls. This person must be authorized to accept the consequences of his decisions.

The third principle is to accept risks when benefits outweigh the costs. All identified benefits should be compared against all identified costs. Even high risk activities may be undertaken when the sum of potential benefits exceeds the sum of potential costs.

The fourth principle is to integrate risk management into planning at all levels. Risks are more easily managed in the planning stages of an operation. Costs of change in both time and money are in direct proportion to the stage in the operation in which they are undertaken.

Risk analysis determines the:

- Consequence (Will it hurt?)
- Likelihood (What are the chances of it hurting?)
- Severity (How badly will it hurt?)

Mitigation is the measures taken to eliminate a hazard, or to reduce the severity and likelihood of one or more risks. Steps in a formal risk analysis are:

- Brainstorming accident scenarios.
- Identifying the embedded hazards.
- Categorizing similar events and hazards.
- Developing a mitigation strategy.
- Determining severity and likelihood.
- Documenting and review.

The following factors affect your ability to recognize a hazard: 1) Personality; 2) Education, 3) Regulations, and 4) Experience. Employees are required to report situations that they identify as potentially unsafe to the company Safety Department for resolution.

A Painful Example

We had an employee who tripped on a floor mat that had curled up. She fell, breaking her shoulder. Someone should have anticipated that possibility. Within 30 minutes, the Safety Department had picked up the mats in the building.

System Safety Process

A Safety Management System that is appropriate to the operation involves:

- A safety policy.
- Clear authorities, responsibilities, and accountabilities.
- All employees.
- Has a voluntary and non-punitive reporting system (*ASAP).
- A company safety-risk profile.
- Training programs.
- A process for implementing change.
- Accident and incident reporting and investigation.
- Periodic reviews and audits.
- Effective documentation.

*ASAP (Aviation Safety Action Program)

American Airlines pioneered the concept. It encourages pilots, mechanics, and dispatchers to voluntarily report safety information that may be critical to identifying potential precursors to accidents and incidents. A three member panel comprised on a union rep; a FAA inspector; and a company representative meet once a month to discuss and implement necessary safety improvements based on suggestions from employees. NASA also administers a similar program for self-disclosures called the Aviation Safety Reporting Program for all pilots; not just the airlines.

Errors Are Inevitable

We acknowledge that errors are inevitable. Most are not intentional but can be directly attributed to poor decision-making and communication (CRM). While SMS is now mandated for all airlines worldwide, many third world countries have not adopted it or only give lip service to the concept. Let's look at the accident/incident statistics worldwide compared to the US. The source is WikiLeaks and excludes military accidents.

	Worldwide	United States
2009	74	12
2010	49	4
2011	19	2
2012	14	2
2013	12	2
2014	14	1
2105	15	3
2016	25	0
2017	111	0

During my 14 years in the Training Department, my most rewarding experience was facilitating the CRM and SMS classes with the pilots, dispatchers, mechanics, instructors, and management. I miss the esprit de corps, and the sincere efforts of the employees who embraced the concept.

In summary, SMS is a quality management approach to controlling risk. It is appropriate for corporate flight departments as well as the airlines.

Note: On a lighter note, you have seen the motivation posters for sale in the in-flight airline magazines. There is alternate universe known as Despair.com which offers demotivation posters. They are hilarious. I highly recommend that you take a look.

Chapter 14

More Airline Stories

July 8, 1987, Delta and Continental Near Midair

Two wide bodies were inbound from Europe about 300 miles northeast of Miami over the Atlantic just outside of radar coverage. Delta was off course 60 miles having entered the wrong latitude/longitude coordinates in their INS (Inertial Navigation System) computers. They missed each other by 100 feet.

The Delta crew asked Continental if they were going to report the near mid-air and that's how the error was discovered by the FAA. Other pilots were on the frequency and heard the exchange.

This happened the same month that Delta crews landed at the wrong airports on three different occasions. Delta was the last airline to adopt CRM but only after FAA insistence following these errors. David Letterman jumped on this and announced the new Delta slogans on national TV.

#10 Delta gets you close.
#9 We never make the same
     mistake three times.
#8 Complimentary cham-
     pagne in free-fall.
#7 The kids will love our
     inflatable slides.

#6 Enjoy the in-flight movie on the plane next to you.

#5 Ask about our out-of-court settlements.

#4 Join our Frequent Near-Miss Program.

#3 Terrorists are afraid to fly with us.

#2 Objects in the window appear closer than they are.

#1 A real man lands where he wants to.

Wrong Turn

The cockpit crew at one of the busier US airports made a wrong turn and came nose to nose with another airliner. The angry female ground controller screamed, "[Call sign], where are you going? I told you to turn right on Charlie taxiway. You turned right on Delta. Stop right there."

Continuing her verbal lashing of the embarrassed crew, she yelled, "You've screwed everything up. It'll take forever to sort this out. You stay right there and don't move until I tell you. You can expect progressive taxi instructions in about a half hour and I want you to go exactly where I tell you, when I tell you, and how I tell you. You got that?" Naturally, the frequency went very quiet. An unknown male voice broke the silence and asked, "Wasn't I married to you once?"

Stressed Out in Chicago

The crew of an American Airlines DC10 decided to have a little fun on "taxi out." The DC10 had a video camera overhead in the cockpit so the passengers could watch the takeoff but you couldn't see the flight engineer in the back of the cockpit. On this particular flight, the flight engineer put on an arm from an ape costume. The Captain snapped his fingers and the folks in the back saw this large hairy arm from the bottom of the TV monitor reach up and move the thrust levers. It then tapped the copilot on the shoulder and he turned and handed back a banana.

The crew had a good laugh and relieved their stress in dealing with ATC, management, and the weather but stressed out a few first-time passengers. Management took a dim view of this attempt at humor in the cockpit. The crew got a few days on the beach (no pay) so they could figure out how to have more fun the next time they flew.

Stress and Heart Attacks

The American Medical Association states that most air traffic controllers and airline pilots will die of heart disease and that most heart attacks occur in the early morning hours.

I know exactly why. You're lying in bed fast asleep. It's 4 a.m. and your wife sits up abruptly in bed and says, "John, oh John!" Your name is Fred.

Snakes

Captain Bob McGalliard told me about flying the Burma Hump in World War II in a C46 transport. They were at altitude when a snake peeked out from the hole of a missing instrument in the forward instrument panel. They emptied their 45s into the instruments. Luckily it was VFR at the time.

Captain Randy Lugar flew the mail out of Redding, California to San Francisco with a stop at Sacramento Metro in a single-engine Piper PA31. One night, he carried an eight foot boa constrictor in a cage and during the stop at SMF, he discovered the cage was empty. A search of the airplane and the adjoining ramp turned up nothing. The snake was soon forgotten.

A few days later, another pilot wrote up a maintenance squawk that the controls seemed to be stiff and the left wing was heavy. The mechanic opened up the wing panel and the snake struck at his mirror. The snake had gone through a small interior hole in the wing root and had been traveling all around California in the left wing.

More Animal Stories

On C130s, (Lockheed Hercules four-engine turboprops), there is a hatch at the rear of the cockpit that goes down to the cargo bay. A crew had an ape in a cage on the load manifest. It was 2 a.m. and the pilots were snoozin' in their seats with the autopilot ON, and the flight engineer was keeping an eye on the office while reading his newspaper. He heard a noise at the back of the cockpit and turned up the lights only to discover the gorilla looking up through the hatch. A loud "Oh . . ." brought the pilots back to life.

Declaring an emergency, they put on their oxygen masks and depressurized to make the ape sleepy from a lack of oxygen and threw food at him. On the ground 10 minutes later, they bailed out the side windows and down the emergency ropes. That's why the hatch on the Herc is called the gorilla hole in the airline industry.

Alaska Airlines hit a salmon at 6,000 feet over Puget Sound. It was dropped by an eagle. Back in the '70s, TWA reported a snake strike at 8,000 feet near El Paso. The hawk dropped it when approached by the Boeing 707.

An airline pilot reported a bird strike. In compliance with FAA requirements, the controller solicited the species. The pilot said he could not positively identify the type of bird, but reported that it was all red on the inside.

The Puppy Snuffer Switch

On the B727, there are two cargo compartments below deck, forward and aft. The forward compartment is heated and this is where you put the animals. We won't divulge the name of the airline but their initials were WA. The flight departed Phoenix for Los Angeles with a white poodle in a cage and loaded in the forward compartment but did not inform the flight deck. The switch which heats the compartment was not turned ON, hence the name, the puppy snuffer switch. Upon arrival, the baggage handlers discovered a dead, frozen poodle.

The passenger was informed that the pet had missed the flight and they would deliver it to her at her home later that day. An employee was dispatched to the local pet store to find a replacement. Arriving at the home of the owner, the lady exclaimed, "That's not my dog. My dog was being shipped home for burial." By now, the original puppy had been disposed, so the company rep had to return several hours later with another dead puppy.

Airline Captains and Other Stories

The 3 most dangerous things to an airline captain are:

1. A terrorist with an AK47 assault rifle.
2. A copilot with a helo rating and an instrument ticket.
3. A flight attendant with his home phone number.

_____

Do you know the difference between a jet engine and an airline captain? A jet engine stops whining when it gets to the ramp.

_____

Heard one night in a dark cockpit: "I've flown in both seats. Can someone tell me why the other one is always occupied by an idiot?"

_____

Captain to First Officer: "Son, you have to make up your mind about growing up and becoming a pilot. You can't do both."

_____

Captain to First Officer: "I would agree with you but then we would both be wrong."

_____

Lady radar controller: "Can I turn you on the ILS at 7 miles?"
Captain: "Madam, you can try."

_____

Captain: "Ground, Lufthansa flight 192 requesting start-up."
Tower: "Sorry 192, we don't have your flight plan. What is your destination?"
Captain: "To Leipzig, like every Monday."
Tower: "But today is Tuesday."

Captain: "WHAT? But Tuesday we are off."

———

Approach: "Flight 123, do you have a problem?"
Captain: "I think we have lost our compass."
Approach: "Judging by the way you are flying, you lost the whole instrument panel."

———

Approach: "United 329 Heavy, your traffic is a Fokker F-27, one o'clock, 3 miles, eastbound."
United 329: "Approach, I've always wanted to say this . . . I've got that Fokker in sight."

———

The German controllers at Frankfurt are short-tempered. They not only expect you to know your parking gate location but how to get there without any assistance. A PanAm crew overheard the following exchange between Ground Control and a British Airways B747 (call sign "Speedbird 206") after landing.

Speedbird 206: "Top of the morning Frankfurt, Speedbird 206 clear of the active runway."
Ground: "Guten morgen, captain. You will taxi to your gate."
The 747 turned onto the parallel taxiway and slowed to a stop.
Ground: "Speedbird, do you not know where you are going?"
Speedbird 206: "Standby for a moment Ground. I'm looking up our gate location now."
Ground (with some arrogant impatience): "Speedbird 206, you have never flown to Frankfurt before?"
Speedbird 206: "Yes, I have, in 1944, but I didn't stop."

———

Nova 851: "Halifax terminal, Nova flight 851 with you out of 13,000 for 10,000, requesting runway 15."

Terminal (female voice): "Nova 851, Halifax. The last time I gave a captain what he wanted, I was on penicillin for three weeks. Expect runway 06."

———

There are only three things a First Officer should ever say:

1. Yes, sir.
2. You're right.
3. I'll take the chicken.

———

A hunting dog named copilot was offered by a hunting club as a rental at an exorbitant price and he was always booked. He would wait patiently and quietly for the shot, then leap into the water to retrieve the hapless duck, pluck it, clean it, put it on a spit over the fire until it was properly cooked, and then deliver it to the pampered hunter. One year, co-pilot's calendar suddenly opened up. According to the owner, "Some dumb yahoo called him Captain and he's been useless ever since."

———

The Union Dog

Four workers were discussing how smart their dogs were. The first was an engineer, who said his dog could do math and calculations. His dog was named T-Square. He told her to get some paper and draw a square, a circle, and triangle which she did very well.

The accountant said his dog was better. Her name was Slide Rule. He told her to fetch a dozen cookies, divide them into piles of three, which she did with no problem.

The chemist said his dog was better. His dog, Measure, was told to get a quart of milk and pour seven ounces into a 10-ounce glass. She did it.

The fourth man, a union man, called his dog, Coffee Break, and told him to show the first three what he could do. He ate the cookies, drank the milk, crapped on the paper, screwed the other three dogs, then claimed he injured his back, filed a grievance for unsafe working conditions, applied for Workman's Comp and went home on sick leave.

─────

Flight Engineer (FE) Jokes

The FE seat on the airplane is the only one that faces sideways and doesn't flush.

It is the FE's responsibility to see that the escape slides deploy in an emergency. It's printed on the equipment, "JERK to inflate."

It is not unusual for a new FE to ask a few questions in the cockpit. Here is the typical response from the Captain to the question, "What's this, captain?" Response: "Works fine, lasts a long time, don't touch it. It costs $5000."

─────

Bumper Stickers

Seen in a parking lot during contract negotiations:
"Don't tell my mom I'm a pilot. She thinks I'm a piano player in a bordello."
Radar controllers do it in the dark.
Radar controllers twist more knobs.

─────

Don't Ask an Aeronautical Engineer

I once asked an aeronautical engineer a question about the Inertial Navigation System and got a 15 minute lecture. Here is his response.

"An INS knows where it is because it knows where it isn't. By subtracting where it is from where it isn't (or from where it isn't from where it is, depending on which is greater), it obtains a difference or deviation. The guidance system uses deviations to generate corrective commands to drive the aircraft from where it is to where it wasn't. The aircraft arrives at where it wasn't, and where it was, is now where it isn't.

In the event that where it is now is not the same as where it originally wasn't, the system will acquire a variation; the variation being the difference between where the aircraft is and where it wasn't. Variations are caused by external factors, and a discussion of these factors is deemed to be outside the scope of this discussion. If the variation is considered to be a significant factor, it too may be corrected by the guidance system.

Moreover, the aircraft must now know where it was, also. The "thought process" of the system is as follows: Because a variation has modified some of the information which it had obtained, it is not sure where it was. However, it is sure where it isn't. It now subtracts where it should be from where it wasn't (or vice-versa) and by differentiating this from the algebraic difference between where it shouldn't be and where it was, it is able to obtain the difference between its deviation and its variation; this difference being called the error. Ah... what was your question?" Author unknown.

Reminds me of Professor Cory on the Johnny Carson Show.

———

A meteorologist is just a common person who went to school long enough to be paid to guess what the weather is going to be.

———

Your Final Exam

If a flag air carrier aircraft crashed exactly on the US–Canadian border, where would they bury the survivors? If you can't decide within 1 minute what your answer will be, you must attend remedial training with me.

———

Life should not be a journey to the grave with the intention of arriving safely in an attractive and well-preserved body, but rather to skid in sideways, chocolate in one hand, wine in the other, body thoroughly used up, totally worn out and screaming, "WOO HOO, what a ride!"

Chapter 15

The P51 Project

Murdo Cameron

During my campaign with the revolutionary composite AMSOIL Rutan Racer, I gained the attention of Captain Murdo Cameron of Delta Airlines who was building a full-scale two-place composite P51, a WWII fighter known as a Mustang. He invited me to participate in the project.

Proof-of-Concept P51

The proof-of-concept aircraft was constructed of exotic composite materials reducing the weight with a World War II Allison V-12 engine to approximately 5,000 pounds compared to the original fighter of some 12,000 pounds. The prototype was retired after 80 hours of test flight.

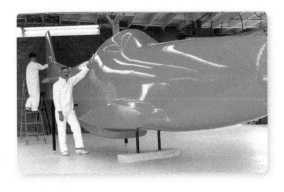

The design incorporates a P51D model leading edge and wing root extension on an H model wing, which results in a faster airfoil. With no rivets, the aircraft has beautiful laminar flow and is capable of higher speeds.

The Second Prototype

For the second ship, composite parts will be cured in an autoclave in Coeur 'd Alene, ID and then shipped to Memphis, Tennessee for assembly. The chief engineer for the build-out is Gerhard Schubert. I will assist as the project manager when funding is secured.

Boeing and McDonald Douglas engineers have calculated that the aircraft is capable of breaking the absolute world speed record for a piston-engine aircraft at 585 mph in their computer projections. The current absolute world record is held by a WWII P51D fighter flown by Steve Hinton Jr. at 531.53 mph on a 3 km course near May, Idaho on September 2, 2017.

Trade-A-Plane, the aviation yellow pages, lists P51 Mustangs for as much as $4 million dollars and those are single seat ships. We think we can sell a brand new, zero time, two-place composite P51 for $2 million. If you're in the market for one, give us a call.

Team 51 Specifications

85 percent of the parts will be cured in an autoclave comprised of 12 major components. The graphite is the same material used in the military F22, V22, and the Boeing 777 tail group.

Engine options include the Allison or Rolls Merlin V-12 (1500 HP @60 inches manifold pressure, 3000 RPM) or the Lycoming T-53 turboprop engine (1450 HP).

Propeller: Hamilton Standard P51 4-bladed propeller.
Service ceiling: 30,000 feet
Takeoff distance: 1250 feet
Landing distance: 1750 feet
Rate of climb (gross): 4200 feet/ minute
Empty weight: 4500 pounds
Gross weight: 8000 pounds
Useful load: 1250 pounds

Length: 36 ft.
Height: 10 ft. 9 in.
Wingspan: 233 sq ft.
Wing area: 233 sq ft.
Wing loading: 26.8 lb/sq ft
Ultimate "G" loading: +8,-8
Cabin width: 34 inches

Range: 1200+ miles with standard fuel tanks-250 gallons
Maximum range: 2250 SM with aux tank-450 gallons
Cruise speed: 350 mph+

Options: Dual controls, air conditioning, large baggage compartment, tilt or sliding canopy, extended wing tips, entertainment system, IFR-equipped, painted to the customer specifications.

For more information, visit www.CameronAircraft.com - 208-640-1620 or

Danny Mortensen at agsdanny@aol.com - 859-384-7821

Allison V-12 Engines

Over the years, I have acquired five Allison V-12 WWII engines and am looking for more. It takes several old engines to make one good engine. Vintage Allison engines are less expensive than the Rolls Royce Merlin V-12 engines. There are only a few aviation overhaul shops that still work on Allison and Rolls Merlin engines at a cost of $150,000 or more. We have a boat shop in Seattle that overhauls Allison engines for marine applications at a cost of about $20,000.

Chapter 16

Aviation Humor

Dear Ann Landers:

I have two brothers. One is an air traffic controller and the other was just sentenced to death in the electric chair. My mother died from insanity when I was three years old. My sister is a prostitute and my father sells narcotics to high school students. I recently met a girl who was recently released from a reformatory after serving time for smothering her illegitimate child to death and I want to marry her. My problem is, Ann, should I tell her about my other brother who is an air traffic controller?

———

Controller: "Is this the same aircraft that declared an emergency about two hours ago?"
Pilot: "Well, no, but it's the same pilot."

———

How do you break a controller's finger? Hit 'em in the nose.

———

How many controllers does it take to eat a rabbit?
Three; two to watch for cars and one to eat the rabbit.

———

What is the difference between a duck and a First Officer? The duck can fly.

———

A checkride ought to be like a skirt. Short enough to be interesting, but long enough to cover everything.

———

If it's not leaking a little, it isn't a real airplane.

———

"It's probably just the gauge."

———

"The weather looked fine when we took off."

———

Both optimists and pessimists contribute to society. The optimist invents the airplane and the pessimist invents the parachute. (Each time I wanted to use one, I wasn't wearing it)

———

Actual Transmissions by O'Hare TRACON (radar) from the NATCA Voice, the newsletter of the National Air Traffic Controllers Association (which replaced PATCO).

"Approach, how far from the airport are we in minutes?"
"N923, the faster you go, the quicker you'll get here."

———

"The traffic at nine o'clock is gonna do a little Linda Ronstadt on you." "Linda Ronstadt? What's that?"
"Well sir, they're gonna Blue Bayou."

———

Trainee: "N07K, you look like you're established on the localizer and I don't know the names of any of the fixes. You're cleared for the ILS approach. Call the tower."

_____

"AirTran 726, sorry about that. Center thought you were a Midway arrival. Just sit back, relax and pass out some more cookies. We'll get you to Milwaukee."

_____

"Approach, what's our sequence?" "Calling for the sequence, I missed your call sign, but if I find out what it is, you're last."

_____

"Sure, you can have eight miles behind the heavy . . . there'll be a United tri-jet between you and him."

_____

"How far behind traffic are we?" "Three miles."
"That doesn't look like three miles to us". "You're a mile and a half from him, he's a mile and a half from you . . . that's three miles."

_____

Pilot: "Approach, what's the tower?"
Controller: "That's a tall building with big glass windows, but that's not important right now." (from the movie Airplane).

_____

ATC: "United 353 contact Oakland Center on 135.60." (pause)
ATC: "United 353 contact Oakland Center on 135.60."
ATC: "United 353, you're just like my wife. You never listen."
"United 363: If you called her by her right name, you'd get a better response."

_____

Pilot: "Good morning, Ground Control, American 2340 request start up and a push back."
Tower: "AA 2340 expect start up in two hours."
AA: "Please confirm, two hour delay?"
Tower: "Affirmative."
AA: "In that case, cancel the "Good morning.""

―――

Pilot Code of Conduct

I will not drink, but if I do,
I will not get drunk, but if I do,
I will not get drunk in public, but if I do,
I will not stagger or fall down, but if I do,
I will fall face down so they can't see my wings.

―――

An old pilot is one who can remember when flying was dangerous and sex was safe.

―――

The Military Flight Briefing

Kick the tires,
Light the fires,
First one airborne is the leader,
Brief on Guard.
If you don't win the fight, win the debrief.

―――

Airline Pilots

Four old, retired guys are walking down a street in Yuma, AZ. They turn a corner and see a sign that says, "Old Timers Bar - ALL drinks 10 cents." They look at each other and then go in, thinking this is too good to be true. The bartender says in a voice that carries across the room, "Come on in and let me pour one for you. What'll it be, gentlemen?"

Each man orders a martini. The bartender serves up four iced martinis shaken, not stirred, and says, "That's 10 cents each, please."

They stare at the bartender for a moment, then each other. They can't believe their luck. They pay the 40 cents, finish their drinks, and order another round. Their curiosity gets the better of them. They have not even spent a dollar a piece. One of them asks, "How can you afford to serve martinis as good as this for a dime each?"

"I'm retired from Phoenix" says the bartender, "and I've always wanted to own a bar. Last year I hit the lottery jackpot for $125 million and decided to open this place. Every drink costs a dime. Wine, liquor, beer, it's all the same."

"Wow! That's some story," says one of the men. As they sip their drinks, they notice seven other people at the other end of the bar who don't have drinks in front of them and haven't ordered anything the entire time they've been there.

Nodding at the seven, they ask the bartender, "What's with them?"

He says, "They're airline pilots. They're waiting for Happy Hour when drinks are half-price, plus they have coupons."

———

As a pilot, only two bad things can happen to you (and one of them will)…

1. One day you will walk out of the aircraft, knowing it is your last flight.
2. One day you will walk out to the aircraft, not knowing it is your last flight.

———

You start out in aviation with two bags: Experience and Luck. When your bag of experience is full and your bag of luck is empty, it is time to retire.

Chapter 17

Calendar Toons

These cartoons were drawn by Bob O'Hara for AGS and used in a promotional calendar which we provided at the trade shows one year. Enjoy.

STABLE AIR...THOUGHT NOT TO EXIST UNTIL LT. CALDWELL C. MOTHERSHED FLEW THROUGH ARCHIE TREDWELL'S BARN IN STORM BOTTOM, INDIANA, 21 AUGUST, 1930

TRUISM 007

GROUND EFFECT...
A DAMD GOOD BUZZ JOB
EVOKING MAXIMUM EFFECT FROM
THE INDIGENOUS PERSONNEL.

TRUISM 033 THE VERY FIRST V-SPEEDS

VTF ... TOO FAST   **VTS** ... TOO SLOW   **VOK** ... JUST RIGHT

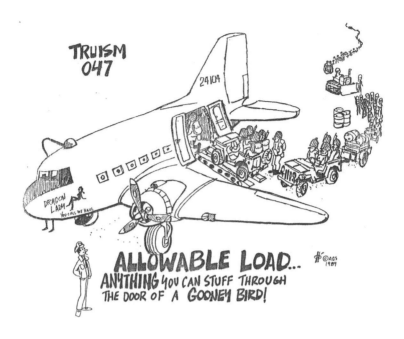

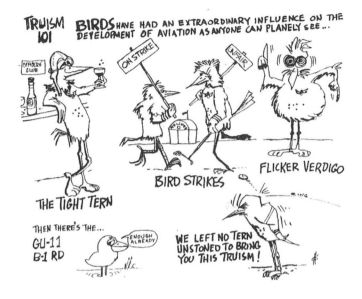

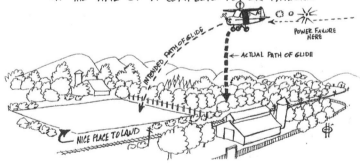

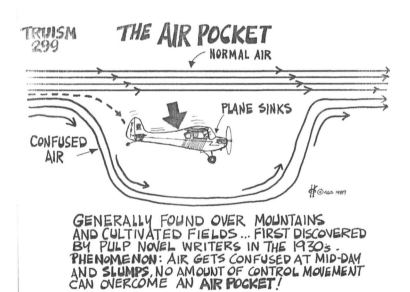

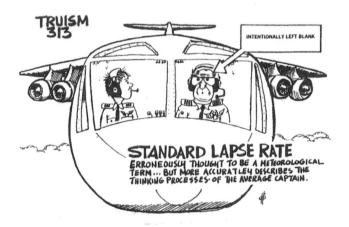

TRUISM 314   WAC CHART

...A MAP SHOWING LOCATION
ON A MILITARY FIELD WHERE WACs ARE QUARTERED
CIRCA 1943

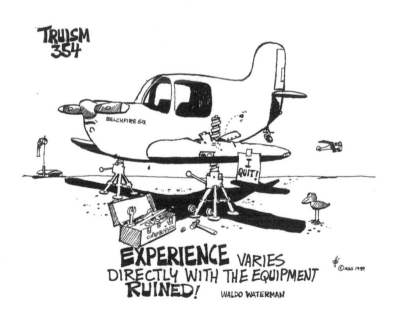

TRUISM 354

EXPERIENCE VARIES DIRECTLY WITH THE EQUIPMENT RUINED!

WALDO WATERMAN

TRUISM 392

MODERATE TURBULENCE

THERE IS NO SUCH THING AS MODERATE TURBULENCE!
THERE'S SMOOTH AIR OR THERE'S SEVERE TURBULENCE.

A TAYLORCRAFT PILOT

TRUISM 399 AIRBUS NO... NOT AN AIRLINER BUT REALLY A BUS!

TIME WUZ AIRLINERS WERE NOT ALLOWED TO FLY AFTER DARK. AT DUSK, PASSENGERS WERE BUSSED AHEAD BECAUSE BACK IN THE '20s, BLACK AIR HAD NO LIFT!

Chapter 18

Reflections of an Old Aviator

Bypass Surgery

In November 2015, I had quadruple bypass surgery at age 69—totally unexpected. The good news is I was able to obtain a Special Third Class medical certificate one year later which enables me to continue flying as a private pilot. I'm going to live forever. So far, so good.

Should I Really Join Facebook?

For people in the "over 70" group. When I bought my Blackberry, I thought about the 40-plus year business I ran, all without a cell phone that plays music, takes videos, photos and communicates with Facebook and Twitter. I signed up under duress for Facebook, so my kids, business contacts, and fellow airline employees could reach me in the modern way. My airline had 550 pilots and I discovered I could care less what they had for breakfast. I also figured I could handle something as simple as Twitter with only 140 characters of space. Wrong.

That was before Tweeter, Tweetree, Twhirl, Twitterfon, Tweetie, Tweeterific, etc. and something that sends every message to my cell phone and every other program within the texting world. I was asked if I tweet and I answered, "No, but I fart a lot."

My phone was beeping every two minutes with details of everything except the bowel movements of the next generation. I will not live like this. I eventually changed vendors and now have a simple flip phone. I don't even know how to enter phone numbers on it and don't care to learn how to program it. The older I get, the less enthused I am about technology. Now I'm not grouchy, it's just that there are too many happy people around me. And don't talk to me about blogging—never before have so many people with so little to say, said so much to so few.

Another pilot offered me his old GPS because he was concerned I might get lost in my 1940 cabin Waco biplane which has no navigation equipment. I don't need a GPS to help me get lost. I've always managed to figure out where I've been. I've flown coast to coast open cockpit with no electrical system and no radio simply using AAA road maps.

You want to know where you are, just drop down and read the name on the water tower. As a last resort, just land on a road and hike up to the farm house and ask. To be perfectly frank, I still do not know how to program the cordless phone at home or the VCR. It still reads 12:00 after all these years (yes, I still have a VCR).

The world is just getting too complex for me. At the grocery store, they now ask "paper or plastic." I simply reply that I don't care; I'm bi-sacksual. It's their turn to look at me with a blank stare.

We senior citizens don't need any more gadgets. The TV remote is a challenge and I mix up the names of the kids and dogs now. I can't afford all that new stuff on social security, anyway. The only thing I do is phone calls and email. Retired and enjoying every minute. I hear the call to do nothing and am doing my best to answer it.

My Compliments to you, if you are involved in aviation, and for joining me in a little light-hearted entertainment, but remember, there is a difference between "involved" and "committed." It's like ham and eggs. The chicken is involved, but the pig is committed. Which are you?

Fearless Froggy Aviation, Inc.

You must have a sense of humor to be successful, hence the name "Fearless Froggy Aviation." After retiring from the airline and selling AGS, I created a one-man aviation consulting company to bring in some money to pay for the gas on the Waco biplane with that big Continental seven-cylinder radial engine. It burns 12 gallons an hour at reduced power settings. That equates to about $85 an hour just for the fuel; not to mention the $2500 annual insurance premium on a rare bird.

I still do occasional speaking engagements, write a lot, substitute teach for Flamingo Air/AGS, and enjoy creating aviation PowerPoint presentations for customers.

Eats flies. Dates a pig.
Hollywood star. ·

LIVE YOUR DREAMS

Biplane Pylon Race Records

May 16, 1976

Lincoln Regional Air Races, California
8 laps, 3 mile course

Place	Race#	Pilot	Aircraft	Time	Speed
1	#89	Don Beck	Sorceress	9:04.6	158.65
2	#14	Tom Wrolstad	Super Chic	9:09.2	157.33
3	#46	Robert Clark	Love American Style	10:01.9	143.54
4	#22	Al Kramer	Too Easy	11:02.7	130.38
5	#3	Dan Mortensen	N1PL	11:31.3	119.76* *DNF

June 20, 1976

California National Air Races, Mojave, California
6 laps, 3.763 mile course, Consolation Race

Place	Race#	Pilot	Aircraft	Time	Speed
1	#32	Dave Forbes	Boo	8:18.2	159.76
2	#16	Win Kinner	Kin-Air	8:56.3	148.43
3	#22	Al Kramer	Too Easy	8:58.2	147.90
4	#35	Don Metzner	Orange Blossom Spec.	9:02.4	146.76

5	#9	Don Perri	Pronto	9:07.5	145.37
6	#15	Red Blackburn	Blackburn Pitts II	9:36.7	138.01
7	#3	Dan Mortensen	N1PL	11:06.8	119.37

September 12, 1976

Reno National Championship Air Races, Nevada
I qualified 19th at 117.90 mph. Only 16 aircraft were allowed to compete.

December 3, 1978

Mexicali, Mexico

Place	Race#	Pilot	Aircraft	Time	Speed
1	#15	Red Blackburn	Blackburn Pitts II	Missing......	
2	#3	Dan Mortensen	AMSOIL Special	Missing......	
Records Missing...					

July 15, 1979

Cincinnati Regional Air Races, Lunken Airport, Ohio
10 laps, 2.3 mile course

Place	Race#	Pilot	Aircraft	Time	Speed
1	#89	Don Beck	Sorceress	8:38.0	166.62
2	#91	Bill Nagle	Mongoose	8:41.8	165.41
3	#5	Don Fairbanks	White Knight	9:03.6	159.01
4	#3	Dan Mortensen	AMSOIL Special	9:06.6	157.90
5	#35	Jerry Maracola	Snaggle Tooth Sal	10:07.5	142.07

September 3, 1979

Cleveland National Air Races, Burke Lakefront Airport, OH
8 laps, 3 mile course

Place	Race#	Pilot	Aircraft	Time	Speed
1	#89	Don Beck	Sorceress	7:09.8	201.02
2	#22	Al Kramer	Cobra	7:28.8	192.51
3	#91	Bill Nagle	Mongoose	7:30.0	192.00
4	#5	Don Fairbanks	White Knight	8:08.9	176.72
5	#3	Dan Mortensen	AMSOIL Special	8:12.4	175.47
6	#8	Clem Fischer	Super Mong	8:53.5	161.95
7	#7	Bert Rathkamp	T.O. Twister	8:55.8	161.25

June 15, 1980

30th Annual Porterville, CA Fly-in and Air Races

Place	Race#	Pilot	Aircraft	Time	Speed
1	#89	Pat Hines	Sundancer	?	?
2	#22	Al Kramer	Cobra	?	?
3	#3	Dan Mortensen	AMSOIL Special	?	154.47

July 20, 1980

Texas Championship Air Races, San Marcos. Texas
6 laps, 3 mile course

Place	Race#	Pilot	Aircraft	Time	Speed
1	#22	Al Kramer	Cobra	6:23.0	169.20
2	#5	Don Fairbanks	White Knight	6:24.5	168.54

3	#3	Dan Mortensen	AMSOIL Special	6:28.5	166.78
4	#30	Bill Cumberland	Hershey Bar	6:29.1	166.54
5	#7	Bert Rathkamp	T.O. Twister	6:31.4	165.56
6	#4	Don Janson Janson	Miniplane	7:13.6	149.45

September 1, 1980

Cleveland National Air Races, Burke Lakefront Airport, Ohio
8 laps, 3.5 mile course

Place	Race#	Pilot	Aircraft	Time	Speed
1	#1	Pat Hines	Sundancer	7:31.2	223.40*
2	#22	Al Kramer	Cobra	7:38.9	219.66
3	#91	Bill Nagle	Mongoose	8:06.4	207.24
4	#6	Bob Hugo	Taste of Honey	8:25.4	199.45
5	#5	Don Fairbanks	White Knight	10:13.9	164.20
6	#3	Dan Mortensen	AMSOIL Special	10.15.5	163.77
7	#30	Bill Cumberland	Hershey Bar	10.55.5	153.78
8	#11	Tom Geygan	Loophole Looie	11:07.5	151.01

*A new race record. Broke the previous record of 208.81 set by Sid White in #1, Sundancer, in Heat 1, Mojave, CA, June 1975.

September 14, 1980

Reno National Championship Air Races, Nevada
6 laps, 3.236 mile course, _Consolation Race_

Place	Race#	Pilot	Aircraft	Time	Speed
1	#3	Dan Mortensen	AMSOIL Special	7:14.5	160.88
2	#9	Don Perri	Pronto	7:16.3	160.21

3	#90	Guy Paquin Buzz	Job	7:17.0	159.95
4	#4	Don Janson	Janson Miniplane	7:18.4	159.44
5	#35	Jerry Maracola	Snaggle Tooth Sal	7:29.6	155.47
6	#98	Bud Pedigo	Pedigo Starduster	8:28.4	137.49
7	#42	Earl Allen	Sump'n Special	8:29.2	137.27
8	#10	Ed Enefer	Super Looper	9:27.4	119.0

September 19, 1981

Reno National Championship Air Races, Nevada
5 laps, 3.11 mile course, *Consolation Race*

Place	Race#	Pilot	Aircraft	Time	Speed
1	#5	Don Fairbanks	White Knight	5:46.5	161.58
2	#6	Bob Hugo	Taste of Honey	5:49.7	160.10
3	#90	Guy Paquin	Buzz Job	6:16.5	148.68
4	#03	Dan Mortensen	AMSOIL Special	6:19.4	147.54
5	#14	Don Janson	Janson Miniplane	6:23.9	145.82
6	#35	Jerry Maracola	Snaggle Tooth Sal	6:28.8	143.98
7	#11	Tom Geygan	Loophole Looie	6:30.6	143.30
8	#98	Bud Pedigo	Pedigo Starduster	7:14.8	128.76

September 20, 1981

6 laps, 3.11 mile course, Championship Race

Place	Race#	Pilot	Aircraft	Time	Speed
1	#1	Pat Hines	Sundancer	5:20.7	209.44
2	#22	Al Kramer	Cobra	5:59.0	187.13
3	#3	Dan Mortensen	AMSOIL Rutan Racer	6:10.9	181.13

4	#25	Tom Aberle	Two Bits		6:25.2	174.41
5	#00	Earl Allen	Tonopah Low		6:32.9	170.98
6	#99	Dave Morss	Mongster		6:34.5	170.28
7	#26	Douglas Kempf	Check 6		7:47.5	143.70
8	#29	Dennis Brown	Scarlet		7:47.8	143.61

October 19, 1981

Texas Championship Air Races, San Marcos

Place	Race#	Pilot	Aircraft	Time	Speed
1	#3	Dan Mortensen	AMSOIL Rutan Racer	Missing......	

September 19, 1982

Reno National Championship Air Races, Nevada
6 laps, 3.11 mile course

Place	Race#	Pilot	Aircraft	Time	Speed
1	#1	Pat Hines	Sundancer	5:20.8	209.40
2	#3	Dan Mortensen	AMSOIL Rutan Racer	5:21.1	209.21
3	#89	Don Beck	Sorceress	5:25.6	206.29
4	#25	Tom Aberle	Two Bits	5:41.9	196.46
5	#22	Al Kramer	Cobra	DNF*	

*Was running last and pulled out before completing the last lap.

June 5, 1983

Exhibition Race, Beckley, WV
2nd place behind Jimmy Miller in his Formula 1 racer.

September 18, 1983

Reno National Championship Air Races, Nevada
6 laps, 3.11 mile course, Racing Biplane Heat Race

On takeoff to the west for the scatter pylon, I was caught in wake turbulence from Beck, hitting the ground at over 200 mph in a 90 degree bank and scattering debris for 1000 feet. Aircraft was totaled but I escaped with minor injuries. The other 3 contestants, Beck, Kramer, and Hines, were black-flagged off the course.

August 25, 1984

Rickenbacker Airport, Columbus, OH

Place	Race#	Pilot	Aircraft	Time	Speed
1	#5	Don Fairbanks	White Knight	Missing......	
2	#91	Dan Mortensen	Mongoose	Missing......	

September 16, 1984

Reno National Championship Air Races, Nevada
8 laps, 3.11 mile course

Place	Race#	Pilot	Aircraft	Time	Speed
1	#00	Don Beck	Miss Tahoe	7:51.5	189.97*

2	#5	Don Fairbanks	White Knight	8:03.2 185.35
3	#6	Bob Hugo	Taste of Honey	9:01.2 165.49
4	#35	Jerry Maracola	Snaggle Tooth Sal	10:02.9 148.55
5	#1	Earl Allen	Red Baron	10:39.9 139.98
6	#91	Dan Mortensen	AMSOIL Dealer Special DNF**	

*Beck had 2 ships and both qualified. Earl Allen flew the second ship.
**Broken throttle cable and deadsticked onto a runway.

September 2, 1985

Budweiser Championship Air Races, Burke Lakefront Airport, Ohio
8 laps, 3 mile course

Place	Race#	Pilot	Aircraft	Time	Speed
1	#5	Don Fairbanks	White Knight	6:60.0	154.30
2	#91	Dan Mortensen	Pacific Flyer	7:02.2	153.48
3	#1	Bill Nagle Super	Twister	7:10.0	150.71
4	#4	Bill Cumberland	Hershey Bar	7:12.4	149.87
5	#47	Wayne Roe	Sulu	7:31.8	143.43
6	#11	Tom Geygan	Loophole Looie	7:45.0	139.37

September 15, 1985

Reno National Championship Air Races, Nevada
8 laps, 3.11 mile course

Place	Race#	Pilot	Aircraft	Time	Speed
1	#00	Don Beck	Miss Tahoe	7:37.9	195.62
2	#5	Don Fairbanks	White Knight	8:24.1	177.67
3	#91	Dan Mortensen	Pacific Flyer	8:30.4	175.48*
4	#6	Bob Hugo	Taste of Honey	9:11.2	162.49

5	#42	Del Schulte	Pitts'N Pieces	10.19.0	144.70
6	#4	Mike Penketh	Passion Pitts	10:22.7	143.84

*I finished in second place in the NAA/USARA Points Standing in 1985.

September 17, 1989

Reno National Championship Air Races, Nevada
6 laps, 3.11 mile course

Place	Race#	Pilot	Aircraft	Time	Speed
1	#40	Tom Aberle	Wanna Play II	5:42.5	196.140
2	#69	Sam Maxwell	Legal Eagle	6:01.9	185.646
3	#91	Dan Mortensen	Pacific Flyer	6:03.7	184.697
4	#90	Guy Paquin	Buzz Job	6:13.7	179.774
5	#1	Mike Penketh	My Pitts	6:20.2	176.700
6	#62	Chris Harris	Sonoma Red	6:37.9	168.831
7	#20	Cris Ferguson	Let Good Times Roll	6:48.1	164.591
8	#4	Peggy Penketh	Passion Pitts	5:50.9	159.514

September 23, 1990

Reno National Championship Air Races, Nevada
6 laps, 3.11 mile course

Place	Race#	Pilot	Aircraft	Time	Speed
1	#91	Dan Mortensen	Pacific Flyer	5:49.4	192.278
2	#69	Sam Maxwell	Legal Eagle	6:03.6	184.758
3	#90	Guy Paquin	Buzz Job	6:12.2	180.464
4	#1	Mike Penketh	My Pitts	6:22.2	175.780

5	#111	Dave Morss	Morss Pitts	6:28.1	173.085
6	#55	Drew Detsch	Uno	6:29.4	172.498
7	#20	Cris Ferguson	Let Good Times Roll	6:45.1	165.846

Appendix 2

Reno Biplane Champions

1964	Clyde Parsons	#11 Parsons Twister	144.57
1965	Bill Boland	#3 Boland Mong	148.68
1966	Chuck Wickliffe	#11 Clark Dollar Special	147.72
1967	Bill Boland	#3 Boland Mong	151.64
1968	Dallas Christian	#99 Mongster	175.13
1969	Dallas Christian	#99 Mongster	184.02
1970	Bill Boland	#3 Boland Mong	177.45
1971	Bill Boland	#3 Prop Wash	181.67
1972	Don Beck	#89 Sorceress	189.72
1973	Sid White	#1 Sundancer	194.75
1974	Sid White	#1 Sundancer	198.17
1975	Don Beck	#89 Sorceress	198.99
1976	Don Beck	#89 Sorceress	202.15
1977	- 1979 No biplane races in Reno		
1980	Pat Hines	#1 Sundancer	206.62
1981	Pat Hines	#1 Sundancer	209.44
1982	Don Fairbanks, Sport Div.	#5 White Knight	172.73
1982	Pat Hines, Racing Div.	#1 Sundancer	209.40
1983	Don Fairbanks, Sport Div.	#5 White Knight	179.59
1983	Pat Hines, Racing Div.	#1 Sundancer	217.60
1984	Don Beck	#00 Miss Lake Tahoe	189.97
1985	Don Beck	#00 Miss Lake Tahoe	195.62
1986	Alan Preston	#00 Miss Lake Tahoe	192.665

1987	Tom Aberle	#40 Long Gone Mong	196.473
1988	Alan Preston	#00 Top Cat	205.918
1989	Tom Aberle	#40 Wanna Play II	196.140
1990	Danny Mortensen	#91 AMSOIL Pacific Flyer	192.278
1991	Takehisa "Ken" Ueno	#18 Samurai	195.273
1992	Jim Smith Jr.	#88 Glass Slipper	193.893
1993	Patti-Johnson Nelson	#40 Full Tilt Boogie	208.466
1994	Earl Allen	#21 Class Action	203.311
1995	Patti-Johnson Nelson	#40 Full Tilt Boogie	202.124
1996	Pattie-Johnson Nelson	#40 Full Tilt Boogie	212.811
1997	Earl Allen	#21 Class Action	198.736
1998	Jim Smith Jr.	#88 Glass Slipper	201.599
1999	Dave Rose	#3 Rags (my old Mong)	210.122
2000	Dave Rose	#3 Rags	209.434
2001	Air racing canceled due a terrorist attack on Sep. 11		
2002	Dave Rose	#3 Rags	224.200
2003	Dave Rose	#3 Frightful	219.181
2004	Tom Aberle	#62 Phantom	237.932
2005	Andrew Buehler	#62 Phantom	230.827
2006	Tom Aberle	#62 Phantom	251.958
2007	Cris Ferguson	#13 Miss Gianna	233.470
2008	Tom Aberle	#62 Phantom	251.975
2009	Tom Aberle	#62 Phantom	236.995
2010	Tom Aberle	#62 Phantom	250.808
2011	Reno canceled due to a P51 accident		
2012	Tom Aberle	#62 Phantom	246.454
2013	Tom Aberle	#62 Phantom	254.242
2014	Tom Aberle	#62 Phantom	225.022
2015	Tom Aberle	#62 Phantom	245.109
2016	Jeff Rose	#62 Reno Rabbit	217.858

Aviation Showcase Speakers

KFOX-FM 93.5, Redondo Beach, California Program log

1985

1. Dec 06 Roland Sperry and Dan Mortensen, hosts
2. Dec 13 Roland Sperry and the Flying Tigers in China
3. Dec 20 Col. Don Taylor, Around the World in a Thorp, with Bob O'Donnell
4. Dec 27 Jeana Yeager, Voyager Project

1986

5. Jan 03 Mac McNicol, Jr., Flight Crews Intl.
6. Jan 10 Wayman Dunlap, Editor, Pacific Flyer
7. Jan 17 Ed Palmer, Dyna-Cam Free Piston Engines
8. Jan 24 Dennis Torres and Bill Worden, Angel Flight
9. Jan 31 Paul Stebelton, FAA Accident Prevention
10. Feb 07 Jim Irwin, President, Aircraft Spruce and Specialty
11. Feb 14 Rod Machado, Humor in Aviation
12. Feb 21 Pete Niley, John Coombs, Pacific Air Center, Long Beach
13. Feb 28 Heinz Gruber, "So We Bombed Moscow Alone"
14. Mar 07 John Baker, President, AOPA
15. Mar 14 Don Downie, Burma Hump pilot and author
16. Mar 21 Bob McCaffery, Aero Club of Southern California

17. Mar 28 Mike Forgeron, Vice President, Analysts, Inc. (oil analysis)
18. Apr 04 Dr. Norman Peterson, Radial Keratotomy
19. Apr 11 Jeannette Rand, Rand Robinson Engineering
20. Apr 18 Dick Rutan, Voyager Project
21. Apr 25 Tina Trefethen, Ultralights
22. May 02 Kit Darby, FAPA
23. May 09 John Kromer, Flying in Mexico
24. May 16 Chris Eberhard and Dick Eyster, LAPD Helicopters
25. May 23 Al Crawford, NTSB retired
26. May 30 Grace Stencel, Women in Aviation
27. Jun 06 Charlie Webber vs the FAA
28. Jun 13 Bob McCaffery, Howard Hughes and the Spruce Goose
29. Jun 20 Tony Levier, Lockheed Test Pilot, retired
30. Jun 27 Marti Vandenberg, President, BenBow Aviation, Torrance
31. Jul 04 Jim Holtsclaw, FAA LAX Tower Facility Manager
32. Jul 11 Judy Scholl, Reflections
33. Jul 18 Col. Steve Ritchie, USAF Mig Ace
34. Jul 25 Marti Vandenberg, President, BenBow Aviation, TOA
35. Aug 01 Steve King, Long Beach City College Aeronautical Department.
36. Aug 08 Arvin Basnight, Director Retired, FAA Western Region
37. Aug 15 Grace "The Ace" Page, Airshow Performer
38. Aug 22 Brooke Knapp, the Aviation Trust Fund
39. Aug 29 Open Mike
40. Sep 05 Thon Griffith, former President, Intl. 99s
41. Sep 12 Part 1. Reno Air Races; Part 2. Rod Machado
42. Sep 19 Barry Schiff, TWA Captain and author
43. Sep 26 Howie Keefe, the Reno Air Races
44. Oct 03 Archie Trammell, Weather Radar
45. Oct 10 Gen. Clifton von Kann, President, National. Aeronautics Assn.
46. Oct 17 Bruce Ross, Aerograms, Santa Ana

47. Oct 24 Don Segner, Assistant Director, FAA (KAL Flight 007)
48. Oct 31 Richard Young, Scale Modeling
49. Nov 07 Joann Alford, Women in Aviation
50. Nov 14 Karen Sherman, Southwest Skyways, Flight Attendant Perspective
51. Nov 21 Paul Deutsch, Polish Wilga Aircraft
52. Nov 28 Allan Krosner and wife, Flying in Mexico
53. Dec 05 R.T. Smith, Flying Tigers, China, "Tale of a Tiger"
54. Dec 12 Claire Walters, Claire Walters Flight Academy, Santa Monica
55. Dec 19 Bill Campbell, Survival Training
56. Dec 26 Rod Machado, Aviation Education

1987

57. Jan 02 Captain Karen Kahn, Continental Airlines
58. Jan 09 John Dill, Flying Tigers, airline pilot
59. Jan 16 Gerald Coffee, POW, Hanoi Hilton
60. Jan 23 Ralph Wise, Unlimited Air Racing
61. Jan 30 Keith Connes, author
62. Feb 06 Bob Crystal, Simulator Instrument Training, Van Nuys
63. Feb 13 Al Krueger, Skydiving, Perris, California
64. Feb 20 Shirley Shannon, Western Airlines Pilot
65. Feb 27 Col. Steve Ritchie, USAF Reserve and Mig Ace
66. Mar 06 Hank Smith, Insights, Long Beach
67. Mar 13 Bob Floyd, Steve Kelly, EAA Chap. 92, Orange County
68. Mar 20 Chuck Pacini, Gray Eagle Aviation Services, Chino
69. Mar 27 Dottie Walters, C.S.P., Publisher and Editor
70. Apr 03 Maggie Wagner, San Fernando 99s
71. Apr 10 Randy "Duke" Cunningham, Top Gun and Navy Mig Ace
72. Apr 17 LTC Roland B. Scott, WWII Army Air Corp
73. Apr 24 Pappy Boyington, Baa Baa Black Sheep

74. May 01 Dave Bean, Director, Western Museum of Flight, Hawthorne
75. May 08 Jack Norris, FAA Western Region Accident Prevention Specialist
76. May 15 Bob Brubaker, Voyager Communications Crew
77. May 22 Helen Cranz, Chief Pilot, Pacific Air Center, Long Beach
78. May 29 Ernie Mortensen, US Navy, WWII Aviation
79. Jun 05 Tom McKenna, Aviation Pioneer
80. Jun 19 Barbara and Kristy London, Barney Frazier Aircraft, Long Beach
81. Jun 26 Paul Allison, FAA retired
82. Jul 03 Nicholette Ganem, Color 1 (the job interview)
83. Jul 10 Randy "Duke" Cunningham, National University
84. Jul 17 R.T. Smith, the Flying Tigers in China
85. Jul 24 Rod Machado, Aviation Humor, Part 1
86. Jul 31 Rod Machado, Aviation Humor, Part 2

Ernie, Tye, and Danny Mortensen, May 29, 1987

Appendix 4

Management Lessons

Lesson #1: A crow was sitting on a tree doing nothing all day. A small rabbit saw the crow and asked him, "Can I also sit like you and do nothing all day long?" The crow answered, "Sure, why not." So the rabbit sat on the ground below the crow and rested. All of a sudden, a fox appeared, jumped on the rabbit and ate it.

MANAGEMENT LESSON: Sitting and doing nothing, you must be sitting very high up.

Lesson #2: A little bird was flying south for the winter. It was so cold, the little bird froze and fell to the ground in a large field. While it was lying there, a cow came by and dropped some dung on the little bird. As the frozen bird lay there in the pile of cow dung, it began to realize how warm it was. The dung was actually thawing him out. He lay there all warm and happy, and soon began to sing for joy. A passing cat heard the bird singing and came to investigate. Following the sound, the cat discovered the bird under the pile of cow dung, and promptly dug him out. Then he ate him.

MANAGEMENT LESSON: Not everyone who drops crap on you is your enemy. Not everyone who gets you out of crap is your friend. When you're in deep crap, keep your mouth shut.

Lesson #3: A turkey was chatting with a bull. "I would love to be able to get to the top of that tree," said the turkey "but I haven't got the energy." "Well, why don't you nibble on some of my droppings" replied the bull. "They're packed with nutrients." The turkey pecked at a lump of dung and found that it actually gave him enough strength to reach the first branch of the tree. The next day, after eating more dung, the turkey reached the second branch. Finally, after a fortnight there, he was proudly perched at the top of the tree. A farmer promptly spotted the turkey, and shot him out of the tree.

MANAGEMENT LESSON: Bullshit might get you to the top but it won't keep you there.

Appendix 5

Abbreviations

ATC - Air Traffic Control

CAT II - Category II instrument approach

CATS - Computerized Aviation Testing Service

CDL - Configuration Deviation List

CEO - Chief Executive Officer

CFM - Commercial Fan Motor; product of Safran and GE

CLRM - Command Leadership Resource Management (United Airlines)

CRM - Crew Resource Management

Deal - ATC lingo for an incident or accident

DHL - Adrain Dalsey Larry Hillblom, Robert Lynn, founders

DMI - Deferred Maintenance Item

EAA - Experimental Aircraft Assn.

FAA - Federal Aviation Administration

FDEP - Flight Data Entry and Printout machine

FE - Flight Engineer

FL600 - Flight Level 60,000 feet

FO - First Officer

FSDO - FAA Flight Standards District Office

FSS - Flight Service Station

GADO - FAA General Aviation District Office

G.I. Bill - Servicemen's Adjustment Act
GS-10 - General Schedule, Level 10 (government pay scale)
ICO - Idle Cut-Off
IFR - Instrument Flight Rules
ILS - Instrument Landing System
IO-360 - Lycoming fuel-injected piston engine with 360 cubic inches
KAL - Korean Airlines
KIAS - Knots Indicated Air Speed
KLM - Royal Dutch Airlines
KM - Kilometer
LAPD - Los Angeles Police Department
LAX - Los Angeles International Airport
MEL - Minimum Equipment List
METAR - Meteorological Aviation Report
NASA - National Aeronautics and Space Administration
P51 - North American WWII fighter
PIC - Pilot-In-Command
PRPA - Professional Race Pilots Assn.
PVC - PolyVinyl Chloride
PIREP - Pilot Report
PSA - Pacific Southwest Airlines
RVR - Runway Visual Range
SM - Statute Mile
SMS - Safety Management System
SOP - Standard Operating Procedure
T6 - WWII aircraft trainer
TAF - Terminal Aviation Forecast
UA - United Airlines
USARA - United States Air Racing Assn.
VFR - Visual Flight Rules
WA - Western Airlines

About the Author

Danny Mortensen
Instructor

Arizona State University, major: Russian – 1969
Infantry Officer, US Army, 1970 – 1971
Air Traffic Controller, 1972 – 1981
Corporate pilot, AMSOIL, 1982 – 1984
Airline Ground Schools, 1984 – 2010
DHL Airways Training Dept, 1996 – 2010

Built several aircraft and raced at Reno – 14 years!
Former FAA Dispatch Examiner – 13 years.
Former ATP, CFII.
Author, radio personality.
Former world speed & altitude records.

CPSIA information can be obtained
at www.ICGtesting.com
Printed in the USA
BVHW092105110219
540030BV00004B/5/P

9 781642 999129